NICHOLAS OWEN

Journal of a Slave-Dealer

D1681019

BROADWAY DIARIES MEMOIRS & LETTERS

EDITED BY EILEEN POWER
AND ELIZABETH DREW

Renan's Recollections of My Youth
G. G. COULTON

Memoirs of Lorenzo da Ponte
L. A. SHEPPARD

Lewis's Journal of a West India Proprietor
MONA WILSON

Journal of a Slave-Dealer
EVELINE MARTIN

Letters of George Sand
VERONICA LUCAS

Letters of Fanny Burney
MURIEL MASEFIELD

Diary of Lady Hoby
DOROTHY MEADS

Diary of a French Revolution Gardener
FRANCIS BIRRELL

Letters of Sydney Smith
NOWELL SMITH

Essays and Letters of St. Evremond
JOHN HAYWARD

GEORGE ROUTLEDGE AND SONS, LTD.

PLATE I

[front.

NICHOLAS OWEN

𝒥𝒪𝒰𝑅𝒩𝒜𝐿 𝒪𝐹 𝒜 𝒮𝐿𝒜𝒱𝐸-𝒟𝐸𝒜𝐿𝐸𝑅

"A View of Some Remarkable Axcedents in the Life of Nics. Owen on the Coast of Africa and America from the Year 1746 to the Year 1757."

EDITED, WITH AN INTRODUCTION, BY
EVELINE MARTIN, M.A., Ph.D.

" I loose my patience, and I own it too,
When works are censur'd, not as bad but new."
MR. POPE.

Routledge
Taylor & Francis Group

LONDON AND NEW YORK

First published in 1930 by Kegan Paul International

This edition first published in 2009 by
Routledge
2 Park Square, Milton Park, Abingdon, Oxfordshire OX14 4RN

Simultaneously published in the USA and Canada
by Routledge
711 Third Avenue, New York, NY 10017

First issued in paperback 2016

Routledge is an imprint of the Taylor & Francis Group, an informa business

© Kegan Paul, 1930

British Library Cataloguing in Publication Data
A catalogue record for this book is available from the British Library

ISBN 13: 978-1-138-99284-9 (pbk)
ISBN 13: 978-0-7103-1344-7 (hbk)

Publisher's Note
The publisher has gone to great lengths to ensure the quality of this reprint
but points out that some imperfections in the original copies may be
apparent. The publisher has made every effort to contact original copyright
holders and would welcome correspondence from those they have been
unable to trace.

NOTE BY THE OWNER OF THE M.S.

The manuscript of this Book was the property of my great, great, grandfather, Mr. Commissioner Marsh, who was a personal friend of Lord Nelson, and Commissioner of the Navy and Chairman of the Navy Board when Nelson was winning his great battles at sea. How the Journal came into the hands of the Commissioner cannot now be ascertained; but it is possible that some ship's captain, into whose hands the Journal had fallen, may have brought it home from Sierra Leone, or, possibly, the surviving brother, who wrote the last pages of the Journal, may have been a protegé of the Commissioner.

F. C. Heath-Caldwell.

Linley Wood,
Talke,
Staffordshire.

NOTE BY THE EDITOR.

The Editor desires to thank the Librarian of the Colonial Office for some valuable references to contemporary literature.

ILLUSTRATIONS

morgen o'Karl

The Atlantic
(on Mercator's Projection)
showing Places visited
by Nicholas Owen

Dublin

Lisbon

Canaries

Azores
St. May

Cape Verde Islands
Bonavista
St. Iago
Mayo

R. Sestro
R. Gambia
R. Sierra Leone
Sherbro
Sierra Leone
(Bananas)

Caribbee Islands
Barbados
Montserrat

Rhode Island
Philadelphia
Maryland
Delaware
Virginia

THE ATLANTIC

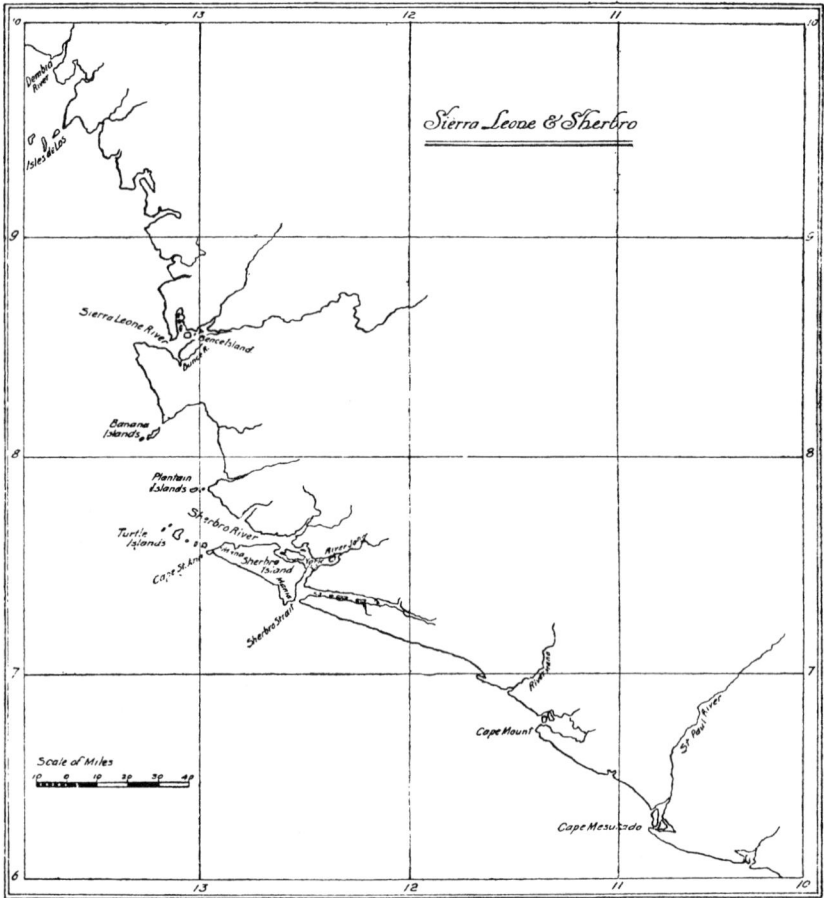

Sierra Leone & Sherbro

SIERRA LEONE AND SHERBRO

Some Remarkable Axcedents

IN THE LIFE OF NICS. OWEN

INTRODUCTION

By Dr. Eveline Martin

THE following Journal is a record of the attempts of
one, Nicholas[1] Owen, an Irishman, to retrieve the
fortunes of his family which had been squandered by
a spendthrift father. Owen has little to say that helps
in the identification of his family; he gives neither
his father's name nor the position of his " good
estate ", and he merely tells the by no means unwonted
tale of ruin brought by his father's " liveing in
granduour above his fortune " and by " the help of
a pirticular law-sute ".

His experience of life as the son of an impoverished
house left Owen with no illusions about the kindliness
of human nature, and as his " hard-harted relations ",
who themselves " enjoyed all the blessings of a
plentyfull fortune even to excess ", failed to show any
signs of " a giveing hand " he decided to seek his
fortune overseas.

In the course of the twelve years covered by this

---

[1] The name appears in the Journal as " Nics ". In the Introduction it
has been extended to " Nicholas ", which may or may not be a correct
extension.

Journal Owen visited England, Portugal, the West Indies, Philadelphia, Rhode Island, the Cape Verde Islands, the Azores, the Canaries and the Guinea Coast; he crossed the Atlantic six times and the " easey seas " between Europe and West Africa three times before he finally settled down as a resident in Guinea.

As the dating of the Journal is spasmodic it is not possible to say with certainty exactly how the years are divided between his various activities, but the period of wandering begins in 1746, and ends about 1754, being followed by the period of more or less settled life in Africa from 1754 to the time of his death in 1759.

Owen's object in writing, as he says in his preface, was to show the dangers of a seafaring life, an undertaking to which he was moved by a " powerful pashon " and by the consciousness that he had experienced " some particular axcedents that does not often hapen in the life of others ". The Journal was, therefore, clearly designed to be read, and careful selection of material was made so that it should only contain matter considered by the author remarkable or of special interest.

In writing the account of his early travels Owen's anxiety to provide " remarkable axcedents " led him to so many digressions that the course of each voyage is a little obscured. The following list shows briefly the chief points in his wanderings:

First Voyage from Ireland in 1746 to England, from there to the West Indies, back to Ireland, thence to Liverpool.

Second Voyage from Dublin to Philadelphia, thence to Barbadoes, and back to Dublin.

Third Voyage from Liverpool in December, 1750, accompanied by his youngest brother, to West Africa. Voyage ended by a mutiny.

Fourth Voyage from West Africa serving under a Rhode Island captain, to Rhode Island in 1752.

Fifth Voyage from Rhode Island to West Africa, thence to Lisbon, back to West Africa *via* the Canaries and the Cape Verde Islands; from West Africa to Barbadoes and so to Rhode Island.

Sixth Voyage from Rhode Island to West Africa, voyage ended by the seizure of the captain and some of the crew, and confiscation of the vessel by natives.

The narrative of these journeys bears witness to Owen's determination to point out the hazards of a seafaring life. Even the short passage from Ireland to England gave him matter for his theme, the misery of a sailor's life, and an engagement with a French privateer showed its dangers. The third voyage in which Owen and others joined in a mutiny against an incompetent captain to whose mis-management was ascribed the failure to capture a French privateer, emphasised the lesson and the sixth voyage ended in such complete disaster that Owen might consider his "Lessons from Experience" well and truly illustrated. The wandering part of his life also provided some matter for his collection of remarkable things. The predominance of the Irish in Montserrat, the tedious length of a passage from Ireland to America of fourteen weeks, the Quaker population of Philadelphia, the goods used in the Atlantic trade, negro kingdoms on the Guinea coast and their manners and customs, the Cape Verde Islands and their products, are all considered subjects worthy of a place in the Journal.

When describing the second period of his life, the years spent on the African coast, Owen wrote much more fully, believing that what he had to say of the country, the natives, the trade and plants and animals was all unusual and interesting. He made no general statement about the slave trade and its importance; probably that was a matter of course to him, for Western Europe by the middle of the eighteenth century had been long acquainted with the trade, and the lines on which it was carried on were well known. When the plantations in the West Indies and in the southern colonies of North America extended, labour capable of surviving the rigorous conditions of plantation life was needed, and the seventeenth century had seen the English establish a regular trade in carrying negroes from West Africa across the Atlantic

PLATE II

[*face p. iv*

to supply that demand. This trade, which has appalled later generations by its barbarity, was, when Owen wrote, accepted as a necessity, though isolated protests were made against it. When public opinion gradually turned against the trade in the last fifteen years of the eighteenth century much was written to show the horror and cruelty of slave dealing, and especially of the conditions on the " Middle Passage " across the Atlantic. These accounts and the opinion they stirred led to the passing of acts regulating the state of the slave ships, and finally to the abolition of the trade. Owen, however, was writing before the humanitarian feeling on the subject had become effective, and he himself took the trade as he found it, a most valued branch of English commerce and one which appeared to offer the possibility of fortune making to the needy. He only once suggested in the Journal that he realised that objections might be raised against it. Having described his own occupation in buying slaves he added " Some people may think a scruple of congience in the above trade, but its very seldom minded by our European merchts.", and there is nowhere the slightest hint that Owen himself felt any repugnance to the trade as he speaks of his work in it as an attempt " to enlarge my fortune by honest mains."

Though he crossed the Atlantic several times with cargoes of slaves he gave no details about conditions on the vessels on which he sailed, a tantalising omission, as his account of such a disputed subject would have been of great interest. To fill out the picture of this part of the trade Captain William Snelgrave's account, written in 1754, is valuable and shows conditions at their most favourable, and for those who want the horrors of the passage there is an abundant literature summarised in Clarkson's *History of the Abolition of the Slave Trade*. Owen's attention was concentrated on that part of the trade which was carried on in Africa. The Africa of his day, as seen by European traders, was a long line of marketing stations, frequented by Portuguese, English (including colonial), Dutch, French and Danish vessels in pursuit of the slave trade, and of a subsidiary trade in gold, ivory, gum and some other less important products. The constant and increasing demand for African labour in the West Indian and American plantations had led to a belief in the slave trade as a great source of financial profit, and the rival countries had fought hard to secure the most advantageous trading grounds. By the middle of the eighteenth century a rough understanding had been reached between the intruding rivals as to their respective spheres. No European nation, except perhaps the Portuguese in Angola, really asserted lordship over African territory, but each tried to make good an exclusive claim to the trade of regions in which they had planted forts and factories, generally under the aegis of a warlike trading company. As the slave trade was not a simple matter of deporting the population of the sea-coast regions, but a most elaborate and efficiently organised trade, dependent upon the works of various groups of African middlemen in the interior, the buying and selling on the coast was a very small part of it. The European holdings whether forts or factories, were not slave raiding centres, but depots to which the traders of the interior, who opposed European intervention in their territories, might send down their slaves.

The English interests on the African coast were in Owen's day supposed to be maintained by a number of forts, formerly the property of *The Royal African Company*, which had been entrusted by Parliament in 1752 to a regulated *Company of Merchants trading to Africa*. There were only two regions in which the work of this Company was at all effective in the eighteenth century, on the Gambia, where the English had a fort on James Island, and on the Gold Coast, where the English and Dutch had alternating forts.

Owen's chief trading took place far from both of these regions; he apparently never came into contact with the Company's officers, and the Company is not mentioned in the Journal.

When Owen and his brother decided to become West African residents they had little choice of place or occupation, as they had lost all their goods in the disaster of the sixth voyage and were in a penniless

7

condition. They were fortunate enough to be rescued from captivity in the hands of the natives by the kind offices of a Mr. Hall, one of the many distressed gentlemen who hoped to make a fortune in the African trade. Mr. Hall engaged Nicholas and Blayney Owen in his service, and acting for him they began their experience as resident traders. The region in which they lived and did most of their trading was the stretch of coast from Sierre Leone to the river Sherbro. After a voyage with Mr. Hall to the Cape Verde Islands, Owen settled in Sherbro. It is not clear from his Journal whether he first settled on the island of Sherbro, or on York Island, a small island east of Sherbro, where Mr. Hall lived, but he evidently moved to York Island at some stage. His brother meanwhile was trading up a neighbouring river, the Jong, where he was so seriously attacked by a " phllgmalick meloncoly disposition of mind " that Nicholas went up river to relieve him and took his place.

After about two years of trading as Mr. Hall's agents Owen and his brother began trade on their own account, and leaving York Island settled " more to the southward " on the bank of a river (see pages 70 and 73), where they built themselves a house in the spring of 1757. It was an unfortunate moment at which to begin their independent venture, as the Seven Years' War led to almost complete suspension of trade on the African coast throughout most of that year.

The trading difficulty was so serious that after a few months the brothers decided " to separate ourselves about a mile distant from where we lately settled, not in any anger or quarell, but for the convenancy of trade ". After making this arrangement the brothers carried on trade independently of each other, though within the same district, until Nicholas' death, in 1759.

Writing of these years of varied fortune in Africa, Owen, partly by his conscious attempts to describe a strange country, the character, customs and manners of its inhabitants, and the trading relations of Europeans with the natives, and partly by the less deliberately made impressions given in his Journal, paints a strikingly graphic picture of the life of an English slave trader in West Africa.

The actual trading with native dealers had in it so little of the remarkable that it is not fully described in the Journal, though illuminating incidents are given. " By and by comes a great troop of canows full of negros with thier several commodites to sell, one fetches camwood, another fouls, a third a bunch of plantains or sume rice, one complaining I gave him no dram, another says as much for tabaco and a third is hungary, another brings his part for service (as they term it) for which I am obliged to return more then it's worth at his departure, otherwise there's a pilavour" (pp. 73-4).

The ships' captains to whom Owen sold the slaves

he had collected by his dealings with native traders did
not always give him the prices he thought reasonable.
He reports the result of one journey from the Sherbro
to Sierra Leone to sell four slaves from which he had
to return with three of the slaves as the captain was so
" nice " in bargaining (p. 75).

During the Seven Years' War with the consequent
losses in shipping and scanty European supplies,
Owen, in common with the other traders on the coast,
felt the pinch of the disastrous decline in trade. In
October, 1757, he wrote of the " terable news this
last week from Sieralone of the want of supplys from
England of tradeing goods, so that they have left of
buying slaves from white traders " (p. 82), and as
late as January, 1759 he writes : " I have never seen
such a scarse time of trade on the coast since I have
known it as this present time. I have not bought any
trade this 2 months " (p. 106).

When not actually busied in trade Owen entertained
himself with such pleasures as the country could afford
to an ingenious mind. The detailed description which
he gives of Mandingo trials and skill in divination
suggests that he spent some time as an onlooker at
these exhibitions, and his collection of information
about native customs must have occupied many hours.
Gardening was evidently a favourite relaxation, as he
calls it " the chief imployment of my more retired
hours, when I think myself happy " (p. 73), and the
furious satisfaction of the English gardener in keeping

down green-fly was for Owen replaced by attempts
to keep land-crabs and snakes from destroying his
plants.

Some hours of happiness were given this wandering
Irishman by a visiting captain who introduced to him
the fascinating art of " shell work ", and who was
responsible for the production by Owen of a creation
which surely would have rejoiced the soul of a Victor-
ian seaside landlady. " I have just finish'd my shell
work and I think it's just shuteable to my dwelling.
It's of a round form with a looking glass in the midle ;
I have wrought it into divers figures with various
kinds of shell and moss taken from the bark of old
trees and shrubs, which I have laid on with turpintine
and bees wax boiled well together into a hard substance " (p. 91).

It was writing his Journal, however, and making
elaborate sketches for it, which filled up Owen's
unoccupied moments with most satisfaction. The
Journal gave him an admirable opportunity for expres-
sing his thoughts on human fortune, and his philos-
ophy is in some ways surprising. Perhaps the most
unexpected of a slave-trader's meditations is the
constant expression of belief in a Divine Disposer of
all things. " As it has pleased the Great Disposer
of all things to convey me safe in all my undertakings "
(p. 21). " I have great reason to shew my utmost
thanks to the Disposeer of all things, Wo has carefully
convey'd me through all the uncertainties of this

life" (p. 63). "It's not what you desire that you should call a good fortune, for the desires of man are vain ; therefore what may happen to your dislike for the present may hereafter turn to your advantage, as He that rules all things lays it out to the best advantage for His creatures. Therefore it's presumtion in a man to lay any blame to fortune because the common axcedents of life dos not fall out to his likeing" (p. 66). "The help of patience and God's assistance Who has miracllously preserved us from the danger attending a seafareing life" (p. 80). "I must be contented with my lot without complaining" (p. 88).

His views on money and fortune makers, though shrewd, are less striking. "In this manner we spend the prime of youth among negroes, scrapeing the world for money, the uneversal god of man kind, untill death overtakes us" (p. 105). "It's not every man's fortune to get money, tho' of the greatest capasity, yet them that's look't upon as dull wretches as to other affairs commonly has the greatest bank" (p. 78). "Europe is certainly the garden of the world, yet there's very little groes there, for a passing traveler for nothing" (p. 77), and his companion pictures of the returned West African trader—the successful, who is called "the African gentleman", and whose "discourse is set down as perticular as Cristopher Culumbus's expedition in America", and the unsuccessful, who is called "the Mallato just come

12

from Guinea ", and treated as " the greatest liar in the world " (p. 77), help to explain Owen's reluctance, in spite of illness, to return to Europe without a fortune.

One of the most vivid impressions given by the Journal is of the loneliness of the trader's life. For weeks or months at a time Owen lived in a little hut-like house (illustrated plate XIII) with no company except that of his own slaves, or of the native traders with whom he did business. His attitude to this solitude and dependence on native company varied very much with his health. In December, 1757, in spite of the trade shortage, he wrote serenely, " As for myself I live in the station like a hermit and make myself contented with my present circumstances since I find it impossible to go of without a dail of danger and risque. Yet it's a dail of comfort to me that I can sit down in my own cabin, after all my sufferings and hardships and injoy the fruits of a quiet retirement, which is a serenity of mind that a man can seldom attain to when he mixes with the busy part of mankind. I look upon the rest of the world as a scene of trouble and vanity ". At another time he noted that he enjoyed solitude because he was " much inclin'd to melloncoly ", and the thought of a sailor's life always revived his spirits by reminding him of the life from which he had escaped " upon that angory element upon which I have been so often tosst in war and peace ", and he reflected that even a poor farmer in obscurity was less miserable "than a saylor who comforts himself in the main top by blowing of his fingers on a frostey night ". Yet between these moments of content were times when Owen longed to be away from the coast "where the inhabitants are hardly above beasts, ignorant of all arts and sciences, without the comfort of religion " and when he was ill his longing was like the cry for water from the well of Bethlehem, so intensely did he desire the refreshing foods of his own land, no longer satisfied with alien fruits.

Loneliness was not the only drawback to the trader's life on the coast. The climate tended to fevers and Owen suffered periodically from what he called " voilant favours ", and when incapacitated in this way from attending to business himself the difficulties of the slave trade became evident. Having no one to attend to his affairs his slaves ran off, and his trade vanished, and with it his hopes of a rapid return to his own country. Yet, in spite of the difficulties of all kinds which beset him, it was not until the last few months of his life, when constant illness preyed upon his mind, that the Journal becomes the diary of a depressed and worn-out man.

The value of the Journal in the history of the European connection with the West African coast is evident throughout, and its attractiveness has been expressed by one who read it in manuscript, and who found it a refreshingly vigorous and simple narrative, reminiscent of Crusoe and Captain Singleton, and of the stuff of which living history and fiction are both made.

That Owen would have desired his Journal to be printed there is no doubt, and though he died disappointed of so many of his hopes he may now somewhere in the Elysian fields be cheered to find that his Journal is being given the chance to save him from the obscurity he so much dreaded.

The Journal as it now exists is a volume 10½ inches by 7½ inches, brown cardboard covered, with leather back and corners. It has, after two blank leaves and the elaborate title-page, which is reproduced as the Frontispiece, fifty-three leaves of manuscript, followed by some leaves which are blank except for the sketches reproduced on pages viii. and 108. There is one single leaf missing, pages 75-6 in the original.

The writing is, for the most part, quite clear and legible, but it alters towards the end of the Journal when the author was suffering from fever. The difference is seen on comparing the reproduction of p. 20 with that of p. 104. (See pp. 16 and 17.)

The illustrations in the original are not separated from the narrative, but appear on some of the right hand pages.

The dating of the Journal is perplexing. As is seen in the reproduction of the title-page, "Nics. Owen, May 25 1756" appears at the top; four lines lower

INTRODUCTION

In this mans Employ Unfortunately to Our Disadvantage
as follows Our ship was changed for a smaller and Our
capt. for a larger in this Vessell we ware alowed large
privilages in the cargo and what we pleased to purchace
In slaves Upon Our return. In this manner we proceeded
on Our Voyage for the coast of guinea again whore we arived
In the space of ten weeks, along passage with a leakey Vessell.

With these Inconveniences we arived in sinalone whore we stopt
Our leakes and proceeded to the island bananas dropt Our
Anchor. the Capt and 5 hands went on shoar in Order to trade
But Upon Our seting ofer silves on shoar we ware secured
By the natives. put into Irons and hove down Upon the
Ground in a Barborous manner striping us of all our Cloaths.
and in short made a prize of Us. We demand the reason
Of such Usage and was answerd that it was in revenge of
a dutch Capt who had forcebly detaind some of thier free
people and Used them Ill. and aded that they would
take Our ship and cargo In revenge but would spare Our
lives as we ware english men this they readeley performd
Our people on board makeing no resistance as being
Ignorant of Our confinement the people they bound with
Ropes. and hauld our Vessell a shoar Confiscakeing
                    Our Cargo which consisted of the following

16

104
Novmʳ 2ᵈ Yesterday arived from Liverpool yᵗ Bee Sno.
175-8 Capt Spotter who I have sould 3 Slaves but
Has not received all my goods yet Upon account
of the bad Surf and bar, I Expect to come by some
Loses as to Wetting my goods before they are well landed
here —————— I have hired some more gremetoes
and find My Self Groeing better every day as to my
health. I am likewise, prepareing for action againe
and exercise ~~~~~~~~~ In this manner we spend
the prime of Youth among Negroes Scrapeing d World
for Money the Uneversel God of men kind, Untill,
Death Overtakes Us —————

Novmʳ 16 Capt potters boat has been here and I have sould
the Mate Mr Eaton one prime man Slave —
in all to Capt potter 4 Slaves for which I received
2 60 Ships bars, one of them Not being prime,
— I have Now In the house Between 3 and 400
Ships bars but Not Very well asorted as to lead &
Iron and Some Other things of Less Note —

25ᵗʰ Capt Potters mate has been here and bought one
Slave fᵒᵐ mr Tucker, Nothing Else Extreme at present
he is gone again down to Mana for trade as Usial,
this Month there is no trade Stiring ——

down the page the year 1756 as the final date has been altered to 1757, and at the bottom of the page the final date 1756 appears again. In Owen's introduction, one leaf further on, it is stated that the pages reached " to the year 1756 ", but on the top of the " 6 " an " 8 " has been superimposed later. There is nothing in the Journal to suggest a reason for the choice of May 25th either in 1756 or 1757 as a final date, but it seems probable from the way in which the narrative is given that Owen composed the account of his early voyages when he was resident in Africa somewhere about 1754 to 1755, and wrote the later part of the Journal much more as a diary.

The entry of August 9th, 1755 (p. 64) suggests that the history has become a diary, and from then on there is much more regular dating of events.

Owen continued the Journal, in spite of his title-page, to February, 1758/9, and after his death in March his brother made a short continuation of it from March to June, 1759.

In reproducing the manuscript Owen's spelling has been left in its attractive originality, and the reader is advised that should a general knowledge of eighteenth century pronunciation fail to make the meaning clear, it should be remembered that Owen was an Irishman and has some peculiarities of speech on this account. Capital letters, so prodigally used by Owen, have not been reproduced, partly because it is not always possible to distinguish a capital from a small letter. Nor has the original, somewhat rare, punctuation been kept. Owen makes use of two forms of contraction : a past tense is frequently represented by a " d " raised above the line, and this is represented by an apostrophe before the " d ". He also had a special sign for " the ". This contraction has been expanded where it occurs and no special note has been made of it through the text. He only once uses the form " ye " for " the ", where he wrote " ye Be sno ", which is seen in the reproduction on p. 17.

Catchwords have been omitted from the text, but a note is given where they occur. All other repetitions of words are reproduced as in the original. In places where it has been thought advisable to add a word or letter for clarity the addition is marked by square brackets.

Where places mentioned by Owen are shown on the maps at the end of the volume, no special reference is made to them in the notes.

Owen's references to pages in the journal have been altered to fit the pagination of this volume. These alterations are shown in square brackets.

THE FIRST PART

LIKE some country swain, who at a ball is charm'd by the musick chearfull sound, fain would shew the meaning of his mind by the moveing of his limbs, but fears the censure of the croud and pines his loss of time and ſtars in laveing him so bare without, when the powerfull pashon haves for vent within and longs to shew by nature what by art he never learn'd, so as it has pleased the Great Disposer of all things to convay me safe in all my undertakings both by sea and land, I should think my time loſt in obsecurity if I sh'd negleƈt giveing a short discriptian of my paſt life and lay open to the world the many dangers atending a seafareing life ; and it's with great difficulty that I prevail'd upon my self to lay my wakeness to the world, or now I should not, only for the sake of some perticular axcedents that does not often hapen in the life of others.

The following sheets is taken from the year 1746 and reaches to the year 1758[1], shewing the several ſtations of life of the author on the coaſt of Africa and America.

The firſt of my expeditions was from Ireland[2] in the year 46 to England, where upon which voyage I observ'd a small scetch of the miserable dependence a sallor has for his liveing, that relies intirely upon the seas for sustainance. The Caribee Isles[1] was my next place of arival, where after the usual manner of unloading and loading, notwithstanding our engagement of 12 or 14 hours with a Frinch privitleer, we had the good fortune to escape with very little loss and persue our voyage to the Island Mountserat, one of his Majestie's plantations in the West Endies, chiefly inhabated by Irish[2] with some few English; its chief comodities are rum, sugar, indigo, cotten and some other things peculiar to these islands. This part of our voyage was taken up with our work; therefore I had no opertunity of makeing any discoverys, nor indeed there was no ocation, as these isles is so very well known all over the world and my chief desighn lyeing in Africa, where I am now an inhabatant. Our stay was short on this island. We took our departure and after a long tedus passage arived in Ireland at Cork and next in Waterford and so to Liverpool, where I staid untill I had refrest my self after so long a voyage and to determine how I should make another to other parts that I had not seen before. This was concluded by my going to Ireland and embarking at Dublin for the city of Philedelphia in North America. Our cargo consisted of servants who shipt them selves volintary for the service of the British plantations in America. This voyage proved long and tedus as the last, being 14 weeks[3] between land and land with continual storms and gusts of wind on the coast of America, untill our arival in the river Dulaware and from thence to the city, which is well built and peoplus, inhabited by Quakers chiefly, a great place of trade with most parts of the world. These people are industrus and civil to strangers; it's under the English goverment. Acording as we had sould our good we recev'd in returns bread, flower, beef, cheese, and live stock. We departed from this continent and arived in Barbados and from thence to Dublin in Ireland in the midle of January, where I settled for some time in order to recrute my self after so long a voyage. After this, Decmr. 1, 1750, I set out from Liverpool in company with my yongest brother for the coast of Africa; without any thing remarkable in our pasage upon these easey seas, we made the land at a place caled Cape de mount or Cape Mount, lying in the N. latd. 8 and lond. E. 7½,¹ a very high land in comparison with the rest of the country there about, inhabited by negros, who is headed by a king or lord who governs as far north as as the river Mana, and to the S'ward this hill or cape devides his dominions from the St. Pauls and Cape Mountserado, another province of the negros very plentyfully abounding in rice and small fouls, which the natives barther for such things as they want with the English who trades in these parts. As far as I could learn this King of Cape Mount is of small power with his subjects in way of goverment, acting as a majistra over them in common causes, and these of importance is decided by a counsell. The character of these people is cartainly

very bad; they are malitiously given, in all thier
dealing decaitfull, great drunkards, seldom at peace
with their neibours or them selves, expert in war yet
ignorant of disipline that [is] used at home; thier
wapens, guns, swords, bows and arows, clubs; thier
chief comodities, elephants' teeth,[1] slaves and rice; they
receve in return guns, powder, ball, dry goods, pewter,
brass kettles, pans, with iron bars[2] and India goods.
After you lave this place you have a pleasent view
of the shoar as you sail to the N'ward, here and there
beset with small vilages and covered with ever green,
bearing many kinds of frut. The natives upon your
aproach generley makes a smoak as a signal for trade,
wher yo go a shoar with safety and barter away your
goods for the above comodities. As yo pass to the
S'ward the natives are more creuell and dangerous, but
to the N'ward they are more civilized and hospitable
to strangers, several white men liveing among them.
We traaded our goods away and purch'd 80 slaves
besides teeth upon this coast, without any other
observations then our fighting a Frinch ship who was
taken by the slaves, all the people kil'd save the capt.
and docter who was ashoar, but without success, for
the slaves behaved so as to make us give over the
atempt with loss on our side, chiefly oweing to the
bad managemint of our capt. and oficers. After this
our ship's crew and oficers was devided and sevare
usage without respect insued, as small alowance
without occasion and and work that was not nececery,

PLATE III

APRIL 19th. 1750

with blows and, to be short, all the bad usage that could be invented both against officers and men. I say this made 5 of us take the following method to obtain that liberty which every Europain is intitle to, as follows :

" There was 5 of us in one watch all of one mind ; it being 4 of clock in the morning, we secured what things was neceery for our intended expedition upon the decks, all except provisions, which we intirely forgot or neglected, and in the begining of the watch set sail, after we had in a resolute maner gone into the cabin and taken some arms from the capt'n's head as he slept, without being discover'd. We set sail in the long boat and stear'd W.N.W., but day soon comeing ware surprized by seeing a boat comeing after us full sail full of men and arms, whereupon we set to our oars and soon lost sight of our enemys, to our great joy and contentment, vouing to die rather than be taken. We continued our course for Cape Mount, being then 14 or 15 leagues distant to the S'ward without any remarkable axcedent since our departure."

Our whole stock of provision consisted of the following articles, vidz. 4 bisquets, a small pot of sugar, and some limes, which was soon distroy'd among so many, it was concluded we one [*sic*] should go on shoar in order to purchace some rice or fouls ; it hapn'd I was taken in the first lot and obliged to counterfit the place of a mate and go on shoar. That being 5 days we had been without vituals I was very wake and unfit for swiming; however the sea hove me on shoar, where I was received by a great many negros and brough up into the town, with a great dail of good nature on thier side, some of them setting victuals before me, such as rice and palm oyl with a foul upon the top. This town is situated to the N'ward of St. Pauls close by the sea, between two hils of sand. Next morning I sent a large basket of rice aboard with some fouls and oyl, wh. they feasted with untill I came on board the next day and set sail for another adventure, laveing the natives behind well satisfyed for their rice. In this maner we coasted along the coast wh. apeared very beautyfull to the eye, thick beset with trees of vast magnitude, under whose shade grew shrubs of differant hews or colours finely mix't. In this part the country was but thinly inhabated.

By this time our provision was almoast gone, wherefore we put on shoar at a larg town, but without buying anything hove up our anchor and stood further to the N'ward, at last comeing to a great number of small islands, which we knew afterwards by the name of the Turtle Island; these islands are well stor'd with oisters and other fish along thier shoars. We went on shoar upon a cape oposate the Turtles and walk't and spent that afternoon in makeing discovereyes conserning its produce; the place was so pleasent that my brother ventured to swim on shoar in order

to vew the the [*sic*] place. We spent some time in
our deversons and returnd to the longboat, that all
the time lay of at a anchor, but to our great surprize
the sea had swel'd so high that Blayney could not
swim of. I ſtaid on shoar that night with him, the
reſt went on board and left us without any other
comfort then a sword and some cassada root[1] to keep
us from ſtarving. In this maloncoly condition we
wander'd up and down reflecting on our unhapy ſtate
untill night, which as soon as come we laid us down to
reſt; one slept, the other watch'd and so by turns we
releved each other till midnight. We ware frited by a
large alegator that lay on the sand close to where we
lay, but soon got up and run along the sand about a
mile from where lay we and so was out of danger;
at day light we discoverd several tracks of tygers[2] and
other wild beaſts upon the sand, very large. Next
morning we walk't down to the boat but no sighns of
geting of. In this malancoly condition we paſt 3 or 4
hours, when Blayney bethought him of a large cask
or butt that we generley kept watter in. In this cask
we ſtoed Blayney and headed up again as usual, makeing
a small hole to breath in, and so with much difficultey
swam him on board again. The reſt of the day we
spent in eating and makeing mery. This ended our
adventure of the cape, which we knew afterwards by the
name of St Ann, lying in the latd. [*blank*]; it makes
one arm of the river Sherbro and the Island Plantains
the other, which more of hereafter. Soon after we

27

hoisted sail and stood for the Turtle Islands. In a short space we came up with one of them, went on shoar and drest our vituals, spending the rest of the day in makeing a great fire among the trees, which took hould of the neibouring shrubs and in a short time consum'd the whole wood to ashes. From this we removed to another and haul'd our boat a shoar and clean'd her, sending over the river to buy rice and so return'd to our old abode, the Oister Isle[1] These islands was not inhabated when we ware there by any thing but munkays and wild creatures of difrt. sorts, well stored with oisters and other fish; they are 7 or 8 in number all lying low, composed of sand with several little chanels runing between each island; they are very pleasently situated in respect one from the other, so that from one you may see them all. Here flourishes Nature in its first bravery without the help of man, beasts, birds and freut has thier full swing of groath and drops each in his season. Here we lived like hermits, sometime on board and the rest on shoar; our chief diet was oisters and rice. In this place I fell sick of a favour, whereupon we call'd a counsele of war to consider what measures to take for our own safety; it was concluded that we should imedately proceed to Sierelone and lay our selves at the mercey of the English governour at the factory,[2] in order for every man to go to his own country and frinds. This we did, and May the 16th 1752 arived in the river Sieralone, where we all took lave of one another and

PLATE IV

THE ISLAND BANANAS WITH PART OF THE HIGH LAND, SIERA LONE

[face p. 29

me and my brother disposed our selves on board a sloop traiding then for slaves, belonging to Rhoad Island in North America, Capt. Willm Brown Comander.

From this river we set sail and arived at the Plantains, passing the Bananas in our way and without anything remarkable hoist sail for the river Sherbro, wher we soon arived. Before I go any further I entend to say something conserning the Plantains and Bananas. The islands Bananas lies 8 or 10 leagues to the S'ward of Sirralone, a high land makeing when you are to the W'ward 3 hilocks (as you see in the draft). It's well inhabated by blacks and some white people, who lives here for the benefit of trade. This isle lyes in the Latd. 7ᵈ 30ᵐ. North and Londt. [*blank*], apear very high from the sea, well coated with wood and furnish'd with all kinds of tropical freuts, such as plantains,¹ bananas, pineaples, limes, papas,² watermelons, and a great many others of lesser note. It's much infested by snakes; it's inhabited by Bulms,³ a nation that inhabits from Sieralone N. to Shebar S.; it's reckned a good place of trade for slaves and teeth, only it[s] wants a good harbour—the rhoad is full of rocks and foul ground. There are several malatos,⁴ tradeing men that lives upon the low grounds and lords it over the rest of the island.

The next island of note to the S'ward us the isle Plantains, 7 leagues distant from the above island, lyeing very low and flat, coverd over with palm trees much resembling one of the Turtle Islands; it is inhabated by only one white trader and his familey and slaves; it has very little produce of any thing but rice; it has a good harbour for small vessels and a considerable trade with shiping. (Se figr. 3.)[1]

1753

"The nation of the Bulums have very little reverance for a devine being, yet sometimes they sacrafice to him for the safe gard of thier houses and fortunes in this manner: they boil some rice and palm oyl, puting it in a bason and bearing it upon the shoulders of the most noted man or woman of the house, all the while utoring in a prayr what they desire; and so, distributing among the familey and strewing some on the ground, thier ceremoney ends. They have a great many kinds of witchcraft, which they practice upon one another as they please, notwithstanding severe punisment that's alowed by thier laws against it. If they are found out they are obliged to drink a large quantity of poyson, comonly caled red watter,[2] which soon puts an end to thier days."

There is a secret mistery that these people has kept for many ages or, as for what we know, since thier first foundation, of great consequence to the pace of the country; it goes by the general name of *Pora* or *Pora* men.[3] These men are marked in thier infincey by thier priests with 3 or 4 rows of small dints upon thier backs and shoulders; any that has not these marks they look upon as nothing. The trew nature of this

30

PLATE V

2 sorts of their danceing priests

BULLOM DANCEING PRIESTS

[face p. 31

Pora is this : there is one among the rest who per-
sonates the devil or *Pora* and before they begin to rize
him, as they term it, he hides him self in some
convenant place within call and upon his priests
shouting several times the word " *Wo Pon*," he in the
bush answers with a terabl screech severall times, wh.
when ever the women or white men or any that's not
Pora men hears, they imadately fly to the houses and
s[h]ut windows and doors ; in a short time afterward
this mock devil apears in the town with all his gang
about him, speakeing through a reed, where he tell[s]
upon what acount he comes, and demands liquer and
victuals from the white man, if there is any in the
place ; after this is over he goes away with singing
and danceing as before and all quiet again. The good
of this *Pora* is to keep people from quarling. If there
be ever so sharp a quarel in the town and any one
Pora man shouts " *Wo Pon*," they must desist or pay
a fine to be devided among the rest. If it should
happen that any person should be out in the bushes
not of thier gang when he is up, that person is toren to
pieces without mercy, even if he was a brother or
father to he that acts devil ; in this maner they have
kept it secret so long among the women and other
people that has not the couriositey to peep through the
wall of your house and discover all. So much for
the *Pora*.

These people are very lazey, seld'm provideing any
thing but just what necery for the pressent, thier chief

diet being rice and palm oyl, mixed with a compond
of herbs and nuts, very nacious to the sight but good
in taste; of this kind there are several sorts which
goes by several names needless to set down here.
They eat alegators, guanas[1] and long worms; these
last I have shown in a draft figr. 9 N[2] for noveltey
sake. They have an inhuman custum in this river of
eateing yong children upon the first crop of thier new
rice they receve; notwithstanding the laws forbids in
the country I have seen some instances of this inhuman
practice.

I shall pass over the rest and shew something of my
voyage to America. In this river we traded till we
had loaded our vessell with slaves and proceeded on
our voyage to Rhode Island, lyeing in the latd. 41 degr.
N. in America, where we arived after a passage of
100 days. In this long passage we suffered much for
want of provisions, haveing 60 slaves aboard with
very little sustainance, our alowance being one ounce
of salt provisions in 24 hours, with $\frac{1}{2}$ a busquet. In
this condition we continued for 30 days upon the coast
of Virgina untill, blessed with a fair wind, we arived
safe in Rhoad Island, where we had all things neceery
for our recovery after so long a passage. In this
place we continued waiting for the spring of the year
and afterwards set out in the same vessell and with the
same comander for the north coast of Africa belonge-
ing to the Portaguese, called Catchew, a little to the
South and of the River Gambia. Before we came here

32

our capt. and 4 of the peopl set sail in the boat in order to fetch a pilot[1] to convey us up the river to the fort. After the departure of the boat the chief mate and I set sail in the yaul to sound, but by stress of weather was drove a shoar some leagues to the N'ward of Catchew, when I made the following remarks :

" We landed in a small bay sorounded with a sandey beech, where the natives thronged down from the town to see us strangers, with great sivilitey conducting us to thier town and furnishing us with nececerys after our fitagues. This town was situated close by the sea and built of mud and stakes drove in the ground and covered with long grass. Thier houses went round like a snail box, haveing many apartments but poorly furnished—thier furnature consisted of stools, calabashes,[2] long hides[3] dried in the sun, which served them for beds, altogather verry poor and main, thinly cloathed (men, women, at the age of 15 go naked without shame) liveing chiefly upon corn and fish, wild in thier loocks, black in complexion."

Next morning we arived aboard, where we found the boat returned with pilot and [sic] soon after set sail for the factory, and arived the next day and moor'd the vessell close to the town under the chief fort (se the draft of Catchew factory, page 34). In this town we agreed with the governor for the freight of the sloop to Lisbon for the sum of 322 moydores[4] to be paid in Lisbon, upon our dischargeing such marchandizes as the said governour thought proper to export, which

consisted of 40 slaves and 3 or 4 tuns of bees wax.[1]
This was agreed upon and we were readey to sail,
when news arrived that a Frinch ship was cast away
at the river's mouth and desired our assistance in her
geting of again or lighting her of her guns and
brandey. This was acomplished in 10 or 12 days
and proceeded on our voyage, but by contrary winds
ware repulsed and beaten on the same coast again, but
soon after, haveing a fair wind, we arived in Lisbon
after a pasage of 50 days, without any thing remarkable
except the carieing away of our main mast under St.
Marys, one of the Westeren Isles.[2] In Lisbon we moored
our vessell close to the King's palace and discharged
our wax and slaves into his India house. It is needless
to give a discription of this florishing citey, as it is
well known to all in Europe.

We departed soon after and in 12 days arived in
Catchew, without anything remarkable but our makeing
the Canaries and coast of Barbary; we discharged
40 soldiers at the factory, all our goods that we left
behind ware in good order, all oweing to the care of a
Portague gentelman named Senohr Pedro de Coasta, a
man of good circumstance. With him we made an
agreement to fright him and his slaves and servants to
the Isle St. Jago, one of the Cape de Verd islands,
lyeing in the latd. 15 deg. North, a 100 leagus distant
from Cape de Verd in Africa due West. We arived
there in a short time and landed our pasingers; this
island was the place of his birth, but upon killing a

34

PLATE VI

CACHEU TOWN AND FORT

a The Govenors house and chief fort
B A Store for goods
c The Insighn
D The Church
E Senor Nicholas dwelling house, or a munry of black Nuns
F
G A Convent of friars

[face p. 34

man he was obliged to retire to the continent, where he staid 15 years, and haveing a good fortune returned to his native country, when the deed was woren away by time in the eyes of the world. This voyage gave me an opertunity of makeing some remarks conserning the Isle of St. Jago, as follows. It lays in the ladt. 15 deg. Not. and lond. [*blank*], very high land frewtful in Indian corn, cotten, sugar and all kinds of tropical frewts. To the S. there are 2 town[s] situated close by the sea shoar, the first Port Pria, the other St. Jago. Port Pria is built upon a preysapace hanging over the sea and contains about 40 houses low built not exceeding one story. The harbour is good and numbers of fish to be caught in it. St. James, or St. Jago, is situated between 2 hills, the capatall of the island, surounded with great rocks and difficult passes over the hills ; the town consists of about 150 houses, with one large church and convent built after the modern fashon, inhabated by malatoes with some old Portaguese of Lisbon, who is sent over as oficers over the inhabatents.

" The carecter of these people is generely observed by all nations to be malitious ill desighning people, crewel to strangers hateing all nations but thier own, a careter rather suteing heathens then proffesers of the gospell."

They are under the King of Portagall, as are all the rest of the islands. Thier comodities are hides and cloaths made of cotten very finely wrought and after

35

the manner of a carpet, a good article on the coaſt of
Guinea, one of these cloaths amounting to 10 or 12
crowns[1] a piece in Africa, which you may purchace at
3 bars[2] or crowns in the islands. They have another
commoditey of great valleue called orzelo or archell[3]
but prohibited to the English. This island lyes 4 or 5
leagues diſtant from Fogo, a volcano . . . or
island which burns all seasons of the year; it may be
seen 40 leagues at sea in the night. Notwithſtanding
this island is well inhabated toward the S.W., haveing
no harbour for shiping that is safe (see the figr. of
Fogo and Brava [below]. Among these islands we
[remained] untill we had purch'ed a good many
cloaths, then set sail, laveing a large India ship belonging to Denmark and bound to China[4] in the harbour,
and in 8 days arived in Sieralone and soon after in
the river Sherbro, where we ware consin'd., purchaced

our cargo and soon after set sail for Barbados in the
Weſt Indias, where we arived after a passage of 50 days,
where we spent 30 days, this being my second voyage
to that island. Our returns consiſted of rum, which

we deliverd at Rhoad Island, our passage 20 days
which made up a voyage of 2 years some od months
and days, every man receveing the reward of his toyls
with honour from our marchant Robert Crook, never
stinting us with any thing upon our voyage, which a
great many people has good reason to complain of
upon the coast of Africa, as he always orderd good
usage in all his vessels, perticularly chargeing all his
officers to be moderate to his people.   This kind usage
and other things worthey the notice of an honest man
engaged me and my brother a thurd time in this man's
employ, unfortunately to our disadvantage as follows :
our ship was changed for a smaller and our capt for
a larger. In this vessell we were alowed large privilages
in the cargo and what we pleased to purchace in slaves
upon our return.   In this manner we proceeded on
our voyage for the coast of Guinea again, where we
arived in the space of ten weeks, a long passage with a
leakey vessell.   With these inconvenancies we arived
in Sieralone were we stopt our leakes and proceeded
to the island Bananas, dropt our anchor. The capt. and
5 hands went on shoar in order to trade, but upon our
setting our selves on shoar we ware secur'd by the
natives, put into irons, and hove down upon the
ground in a barborous manner, striping us of all our
cloaths, and in short made a prize of us.   We demand
the reason of such usage and was answer'd that it was
in revenge of a Dutch capt.[1] who had forcebly
detain'd some of thier free people and used them ill,

37

and aded that they would take our ship and cargo in revenge but would spare our lives, as we ware English men. This they readeley perform'd, our people on board makeing no resistance as being ignorant of our confinement. The people they bound with ropes and hauld our vessell ashoar, confistacateing our cargo which consisted of the following goods—rum, tabaco, sugar, chocolate, snuff, and houshould furniture— drank and eat untill they ware easey, rifleing our chests and plundering us of every thing they thought proper. In this adventure we lost 4 years' pay all in gold, besides our venture which amounted to 40 or 50 dollars[1] in New England, and consequently a great dail more in Africa. We ware detain'd in irons 4 or 5 days, when they let us have libertey to walk up and down the island for our recreation. In this maner we remain'd, untill a certain gentelman named Mr. Hall caried us of the island in his shalop, he being the same time bound the Cape de Verd islands, in order to buy cloaths, such as I have spoken of before in the begining of my Journal. This gentelman was one who has, like a great many others, spent his estate at home, therefore obliged to go abroad in search of a new one, one of these who goes by general name of a good fellow, that dispizes all who shrinks his shoulders at that generous spirit of liberality, one who said in his hart " let tomorow provide for it self " and to conclude he had a good many principles of honour, yet mix't with some stains that made his charectter jubus. I say with this man we ware engaged in the quality of traders and, haveing occation for a navagator to show him his way to the islands, we became more serviceable to our new master then he expected. From this isle we took our departure, our sloop's company consisting of 3 white men, vid. me and my brother with our master besides 10 or 12 black saylors, commonly known by the name of gremetoes,[1] free people who volonterely went with us in our expedition for a a small demand of wages, not amounting to above 2 crowns pr. month. In this manner we set out for Brava, however we ware obliged to put in to the river Gambia for provisions, where we ware well recev'd and in June 14 push'd on our voyage for the island, tutching in our way at Goree, a Frinch factory[2] on that coast and considerable strong. 7 days after we arived among the Cape de Verd islands, sailing along by the Isle of May,[3] St. Jago and Fogo. The latter burns continualy at the top and is very dreddfull in the night to saylors (see figr. plate[4]).

Under the lee of this island we ware becalm'd 6 or 7 days, notwithstanding a strong gale out at sea, in which time took up a boat in distress belonging to Brava. These people ware in a miserable condition, haveing nothing on board save 1 bunch of bananas and 3 or 4 baskets of pittatoes, with some gords full of fresh water; thier boat was leakey and sails all tore; in this condision ware these poor people when we bore down upon them with our sloop, being then 8 or 9

39

leagues dist. from any of the islands. We receved them on board, being 8 in number. They were bound to Fogo, but by stress of weather ware driven where we found them. Soon after we gain'd our port not without the loss of the Portague boat.

It's impossable to say how much these people made of us in thier own island, shewing us all the marks of gratitude that simple people could, loading us with pressents such as the island produc'd and the blessings of thier wives and children for saveing thier husbands and fathers from death. I have no whare seen people so hospitable to strangers, considering they are Portagues, as these of Brava and the differance of the inhabatents of these islands. In St. Jago the natives are proud and great theves, a charrecter peculuar to the Portague nation. In Brava the inhabatants are simple, good natured and full of respect to strangers ; they are chiefly of a malata colour and are under the Portague goverment. They have one magestrate or governour, who desides causes, and, as in other places, it's a place that's very little frequented by other nations, which is the occation of its simplisity of manners. This island is blessed with all kinds of sustanance for the life of man. Thier chief commodities are fine cloaths, beef, pork, turkeys and all kinds of tame foul, with goats and other things of small value at easey prices, and orzelo that famous weed for dyers' use. I have often thought that if ever I should think of settling out of my native country that Brava should be the place. As for beef and pork, it's sould cheaper her than in any part of Urope. Upon your aproach to this place you would think it impossable to live upon sich an hape of ſtones; it's surrounded with rocks of a wondrous hight. Upon your ascending these hills you'll see pleasent vallies, cool air with summer almoſt all the year, ripe freuts; it has 2 safe harbours, the one called Furno, the other Fashon de Agua. They have a small town on a pleasent valie, where they live in small houses of stone badly built and furnished. This place produces wine. In this place we disposed of our cargo which consiſted of the following articles :

White linnen,
Slazes,¹ small slaves, [*sic*].
Callico and India goods,
Rum and powder, guns basons and knives,
Snuff—thier returns are h. cloaths of all kinds and orzelo, live ſtock and wine.

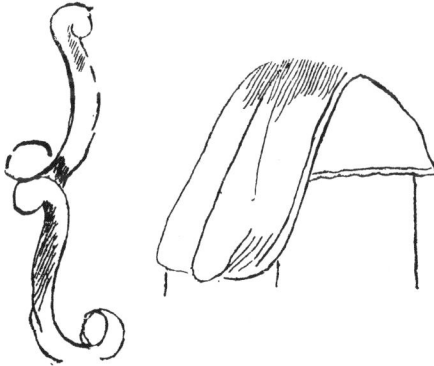

After we had disposed of our good and recev'd our returns, we took lave of these people, not without an earnest invitation of returning next year, sending us several pressants down to the sloop at our departure ; and so we set sail bearing away for the coast of Africa. You'll see in the above a draft a place where we anchor'd, under the high land of Fogo, which for its dreadfull situation I have taken down as in the draft above.

June the 12th we arived on the coast, first at Sieralone, and 3 days after at the Plantains, where we endeavour'd to sell these cloaths at the best advantage to the natives and desighn'd as soon as our barter was over to make another voyage [to] the islands ; but some domestic troubles has put a stop to our expedition, therefore I return to my former history of the coast of N. Guinea. To fill up my paper I shall give a discriptian of our master's adventures among the islands of Bibsequess, some 60 or 70 leagues to the N'ward of where we live.

The adventures of Mr Richard Hall on the islands of Bibsequess on the North coast of Africa, in the latd. 10 degr. 30 North.

In the year [*blank*] upon a voyage from London we found our selves in the latd. 14 and the same day made the land of Cape Verd ; being then becalm'd, our long boat was ordred out to discover more plainer the

42

PLATE VII

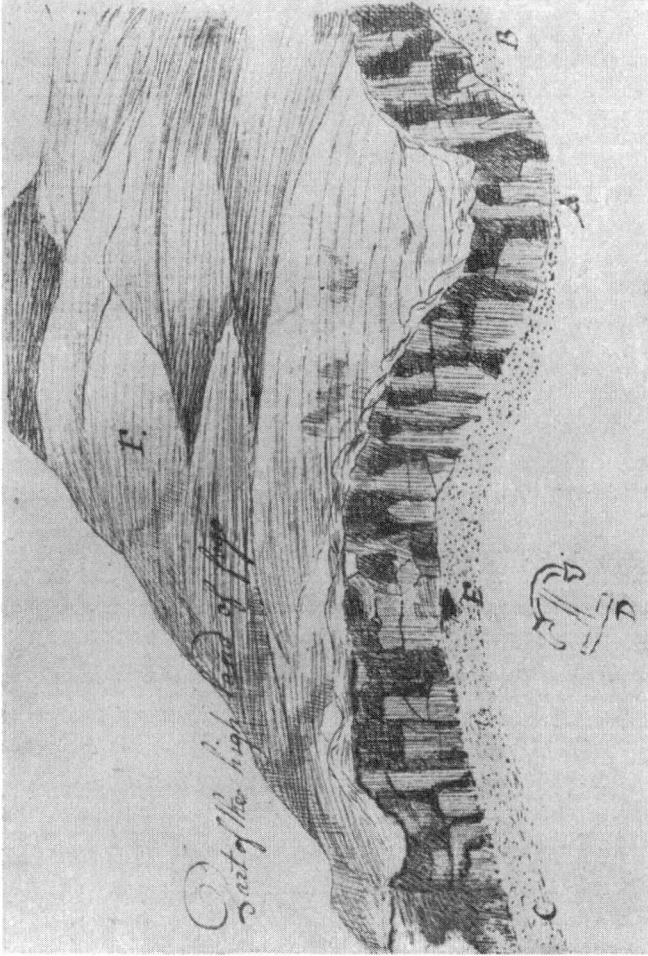

PART OF THE HIGH LAND OF FOGO

A A cape
B A sandey bay
C Another cape

D Anchoring place
E Watering place
F The high land

[face p. 42

PLATE VIII

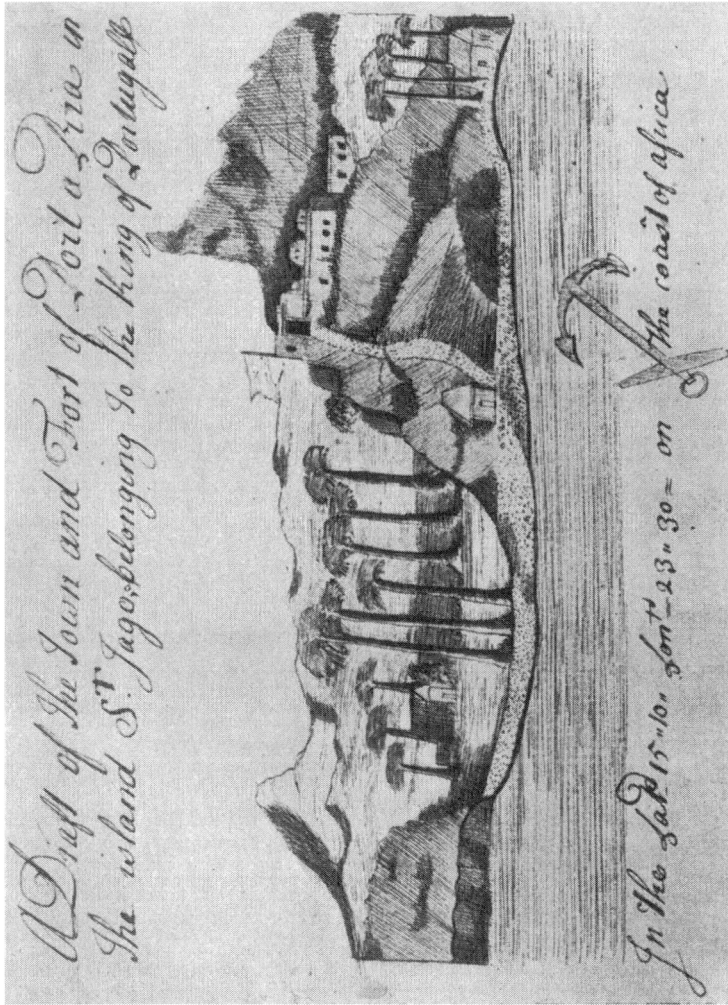

A Draft of the Town and Fort of Port a Pria in the island Sᵗ Jago, belonging to the King of Portugall

In the Latᵗ 15" 10' Lonᵗ 23" 30' on the coast of africa.

THE TOWN AND FORT OF PORT-A-PRIA

[face p. 43

Cape. I was one who had a desire to see what I never had seen before, therefore I stept into the boat with some gentelmen of my aquantaince. We set sails and oars untill we ware close to the shoar, but the calm still continueing night came on and after 3 or 4 hours it begun to blow hard, which parted us so far from the ship that we lost her by the morning and after a long needless search we ware obliged to shif for our selves, stearing down the coast to the S'ward. Our provisions consisted of salt beef and bread, with a small quantity of water. As none of us was ever on the coast before we never knew that we ware so near an English castle¹ as Gambia, but steared away before the wind untill our fresh water was gone, which misfortune obliged us to keep close by the shoar in order to suply our wants, but to no purpose; the natives came down in throngs, which frighted us from going on shoar. We continued in this condition when we found our selves abrest of a parcell of islands, where we ware cast away in the night by ventureing the boat a shoar to get water, our boat being stove by the sea and us at the mercy of the barborous natives. Upon this island we lived undisturbed for a considerable time, where we found shades² that belonged to the fishermen of other islands, untill we ware taken by the natives, after we had lived 5 months without seeing any of the inhabetents. This island was frequented but once in the year by the blacks and upon thier randesvoze as usual we became thier

43

pray. There was a long debate wheather or no to kill us or save our lives, as far as we could understand by sighns, but upon our submiting in all respects we ware preserved to better fortune. Imedatly we ware separated by pairs and me and my companion was caried to the King of the country; as for the rest of our company I could never lern how they ware disposed: As for me and my partner they treated very cively, but in a short time I lost my partner and could never know how he came to escape, as he did as he was seen afterward on board a ship at Siera Lone. In a short time I was aquainted with thier language and therefore became more axceptable to every bodey. It was agreed that every houshoulder should pay me a small measure of pulse everyday, with a horn of palm wine and a good quantity of fish, sometimes flesh, and milk without measure. I was the chief favorate of the King, who to shew his affections toward me maried me to one of his daughters and made me a pressent of a large white cow to ride upon to receve my dayly alouance from the¹ natives. I still grew more and more in every bodey's favour as I was a doctor by preffesion and had good fortune to make some cures of my nabours. My greatest want was wareing aperell. I was obliged to ware bretches of goats' skins, as for shirts I had none or [sic] any kind that wasn't made of hides undrest. In this this condition, I spent three years nine months and some odd days without seeing the face of a white man, when

a white gentelman from Sieralone was tradeing in the
river of Renonas[1] and, heareing by some of the people
that there was a white man in the Bibsequess, sent his
people for me with a present to the King. But with
great difficultey I was suffer'd to depart not without
solmn protestations of returning. I soon arived at
the river, where I was entertain'd like a gentelman and
with joy reflected on my past slavery and pressent
hapyness.

FINIS

We are now to return to our history of Sherbrow
where I am now an inhabatent. Our chiefest busness
is in the purchaceing of slaves, which is very troublesome. In the first place you are obliged to treate them
all to liquer before you purchase anything or not ; at
the same time you are liable to thier noise and bad
langague without any satisfaction. You are obliged
to take all advantages and lave all bounds of justice
when tradeing with these creatures as they do by you,
otherwise your goods ont fetch thier starling price
at home. Some people may think a scruple of
congience in the above trade, but it's very seldom
minded by our European merchts. Our common
goods here for a prime slave is as follows—ships'
boats indeed give more—goods for a slave up the
river Sharbrow in the year 1755 (country money)
stands thus[2] :

C— Bars		Which changed into ship's bars stands thus :		
			Bars	S	D
4 guns	20	4 guns	16	0	0
2 kegs bowder	6	2 kegs powder	4	0	0
1 piece blew baft[1]	10	1 baft	6	0	0
1 kettle	4	1 kettle	2	2	6
2 brass pans	2	Bs. pans	1	2	8[2]
1 duzn. knives	1	Dzn. knives	0	4	6
2 basons	2	2 basons	1	2	6
2 iron bars	2	2 iron bars	2	0	0
1 head beads	1	5 flints	0	2	0
50 flints	1	1 silk handr.	1	0	0
1 silk handk.	1	1 head beads	0	3	4
Country bars	20	Ships bars	36	1	6

This is the general goods on the coast of Guinea for slaves, considering your price in the country when sould on board this pressent year which is B.80, so that your prfits is coniderable if the price stands with shiping. Dye wood is much the same in trade, commonly giveing 3 country bars pr. quentall[3] or 112[11], which will amount to 6 on board a ship ; but these proffits are brought down by the expences of the kings and you[r] own people, which is verey unreasonable and great : as for example, in Sherbro there is 3 kings who divides the country among them, vizd. K. Sherbro, King Shefra, K. Sumana and some others of less note ; every one of these expects custum from a white trader or ships boat, which comes to 14 or 20 bars each at your first comeing and after perhaps 10 or 12 bars, if you bring a shallop or long boat. I say this takes considerably of your proffits away.

PLATE IX

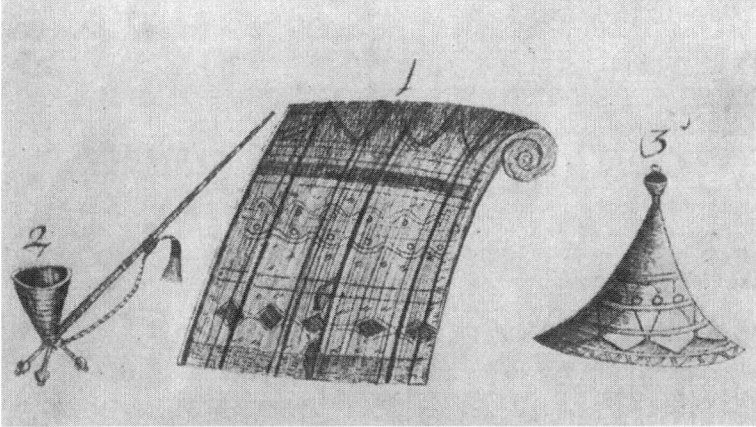

NATIVE MAT, PIPE AND LAFFA

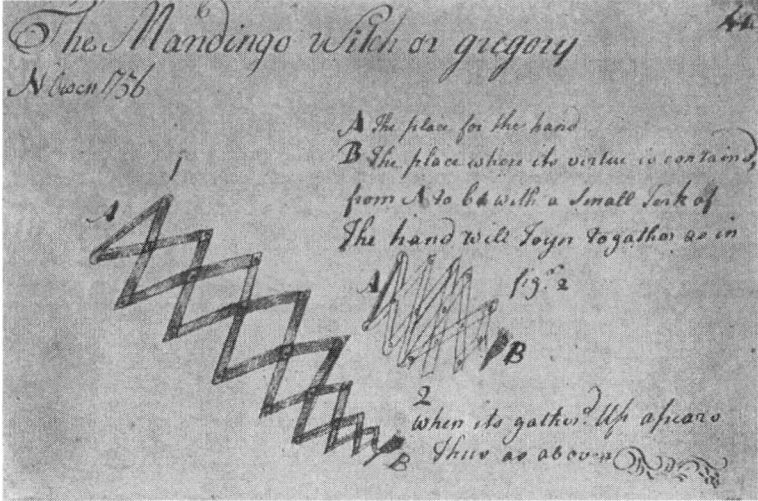

THE MANDINGO WITCH OR GREGORY

These kings are headed by the King of Sherbro, who seems to have the moſt power in these parts ; he is an old man heal of bodey and in everything as formerly save the loss of sight ; he lives upon the island of St. Ann,[1] in the river Sherbro, part of his dominions reaching as far as the Banas [*sic*], where every year he sends his cano for dutey, a certain tribute he's intitle[d] to from the inhabatents of the above places.

These people that goes by the names of kings and princes are only so in title. Thier subſtance consiſts of nothing more then a lace hat, a gown and a silver-headed cane and a mat to sit down upon, which serves to diſtingush them from the reſt of the negros. Indeed they are atended by a good many people when they go to see any white man, who follows them for sake of what they can extort from us. In this light they apear to me, they are people of no magnificence or grandour, their greateſt men wareing a gown, or large garment of loose cotten cloath, with drawers of the same ; they are much given to ſtrong liquers and the use of tobaco, some haveing pipes that will hould a quart with a reed 4 or 5 feet long to convey the smoak to the mouth. There is something that God alows us perticularly from these people, which religion bring into us which they can never attain to without it ; religion would clear thier underſtanding and endo them with principels of honour and honeſtey toward one and other. It seem ſtrange that here in this country you'll find men of ready wit in all thing relateing to comon

47

busness, yet if they [are] queston'd conserning a future
state they give up all pertentions to humanity and
wander in absurities as black as thier faces. They
laugh [at] one and others misfortunes and don't seem
to repine at thier own, given to drunkiness and
quarling, very cowardly and great boasters, miserably
poor in general and live low as to vituals, soon provoked
to anger and soon made up again if the offender makes
an acknoledgement of his crime or pays, otherwise
it's never at an end.

This place affordeth palm wine and oyl out of the
same tree, with nuts and cabage. There are 2 sorts
of palm trees, one long the other short; the long tree
is smoth up to the top without branches and produces
sweet wine, the other bears branches all the way up,
the wine it produces is tartish and not so good as the
other. This liquer is good for nothing if kept 24 hours,
looseing both its taste and smell; it's very chape
and plentey in these parts.

Laws

Thier laws is of little or no force on a white man's
side, yet they'll make a show of justice in order to draw
liquer or goods from you if possable. If they see you
are poor they quite neglect you, otherwise if rich
almost any crime may be bought of except whts.
against the *Pora* spoken of before, every thing else may
be bought of. They seldom take your life, if you
have money to redeem yourself, as they call all sorts

of goods. Any part of speech that is spoken against a man, let it be ever so little, if the person hears it it's called a pilaver[1] and demands satisfaction in money before your are recconcil'd again. Among themselves they send for the king upon an affair of importance and some of the old men, who desides the cause ; the partey consern'd is prohibited to spake in his own affair. Whatever the king and his counsell gives is taken for justice among these people without murmuring and so their lawsute ends. In case the king is indispos'd they call 4 or 5 of the heads men of the town where they belong and sits as a jury and administers justice. This is all that these people has to keep pace among them in the way of grevances between man and man, except the *Pora* as before.

RELIGON

As I have said before there is little or no religon among these people, therefore conscience is but a small burden in Sherbro. Not to say that they are altogather destatute of it neither, for they belive that there is a god who has made the world and all things, but they never worship him in any set place, or honour him more then by sacraficeing once or 2 a year, giveing more honour to thier idols or devils then they do a devine being, which consist only of some old glass bottles, or bones of an alegator, sheep, or goat, which they visit some times with reverance, as you see in the figr. of thier pagods (divil houses). They have great leather bags contains thier witches or idols, which they carey about upon all ocations, thinking thereby to preserve themselves from shot, knives, poyson or other axcedents of life; these bags goes by the name of gregory bags[1]; they are made up in the country and is esteemd very much in these places [plate x] places [*sic*] for thier singular virtue of preserveing the person wo bears them. In thier opinions it's impossable to hurt a man that has one of these bags about him, which occations them to apear more resolute in the face of thier enemys, tho' indeed at the best thier courage is but small. If any of them is hurt with with one of these about him and is demanded why his witch could not preserve him, he answers that he has been negletfull in his sacraficeing, or some other nonsense that serves as an excuse, for fear of dominishing the virtue of his bags or gods, for in case of necesety he sels them to any of his aquaintance who wants, or lends them upon any ocation. These relects are the chief of thier worship upon all ocations, so that I find no nation now so far from truth, except the Hotentots on the Cape of Good Hope, or the Indians in America. In India there are some gross adolitars indeed, but not so foolish in thier manner of worship, as they have set times for worship and are more pious, spending great part of thier lives in the worship of whatever dietey they reverance. Here it's not so: they very seldom are seen to make any shew of reverance to any of thier

50

PLATE X

A Large gregory bag or witch
B A sect of their priest called Tasso

[face p. 50

devils, but when in common discourse he may perhaps say that his witch perhaps exceds all that ever he has seen, to make it the more precious in the eyes of the world, or some such stuff. The women commonly sacrafice at the new moon to thier houshould gods, as in the first part of my book. This is all that needfull to be said of the nation of the Bulums conserning religon.

Manner of liveing of the blacks up Sharbro. Thier houses are built of wood and mud thatched overhead with grass or leaves of treese, ill furnish'd and poor yet they seem comfortable as they are always neat and clean, spread round with mats to keep out vermin or could in the nights. Upon these mats the natives lie upon a bed or cabbin of sticks and curtains of mats hanging down to the ground; in this manner they live as to houses. As thier furniture are suteable to the house, its propper they should be menton'd, which consists of stools and earthen pots of the country make with some old bags of grass or cloath to hould the good man's tabaco or *cola,[1] ivory spoons and cargo knives; this is commonly what is to bee found in a gentelman's house on this part of the coast of Africa. Thier diet is rice, palm oyl and small fouls at thier common meals. Other times they have wild dear, monkays, elephants, alegators and several kinds of fish and birds, but the most perticular kind of food is large worms[2] that groes in trees clos to the water, some

* a frut they have in Guinea.

51

exceeding 3 inches long and as thick as a man's thumb, of colour white and hideous to behold, notwith-standing they are good eateing and fat; these are call'd by the natives *Hant* in thier langauge. Thier chief deversions is playing upon a certain instrument of wood which sounds like a bad fidle; this instrument is called a *Bangelo*[1]; they have likewise drums and other games or exercises of deversion. As for fishing and fowling they esteem as hard work.

The women in Africa commonly undergoes the hardest of the labour, makeing plantations and beating out the rice (for they have no mills as in other places) the same time the men are smoaking thier pipes, or danceing at home in thier houses, or drinking palm wine under some shade in the bushes. They keep thier women very much under and will never allow them to eate at one table with thier husbands; all the time he's eating shee stand[s] by with water to to serve him and so upon all occasions she waits like a servant upon her husband at home and abroad. There is one thing very perticular in Sherbrow as to the burials of thier dead, the corps is kept 7 or 8 days before they put him in the ground, all the while fireing of guns and makeing mery; this they call crying for thier departed frinds. Any white man that neigh hand, he is obliged to send some small matter to shew he's consern'd, such as a bottle of rum or fathom of cloath or some such matter. After this is all over in 4 or 5 years the relects of the person is taken out of the

52

ground again if he was of any great repute when liveing, and the same ceremony used again to retain his memory as if he died yesterday. These and a great many other customs are used by these people that's hardly worthey of seting down, such as thier marages. If a man in these parts takes a fancey to any of his neibours' daughters, he must take a small pressent and go and see the father or guardian of the girl; in the main time he breaks his mind to him conserning his daughter; if the perposial is liked the old man summons some of his old aquaintance and the girl and the match is made acording to the father's consent. In the mean time the gallant goes home again and gathers amongst his frinds as much as his abilities will allow, some times 30 to 40 bars; this he gives to her father and his friends and the girl is deliver'd to him as his wife or rather, in my opinion, his slave. This is all the form of that ceremoney in these parts of Africa; as for the inland parts I have not yet learn'd, only as to thier respective nations which stands thus by thier own acount. To the eastward of the Bulums lies the nation of the Timnes or Timines,[1] which seems by thier quantity of slaves to be a peopleous nation; this nation speakes a langauge of thier own far diffr't from the Bulums, but I am not able to give any acount, as they lie so far inland and as we have no tradeing among them. Next to these inland is the Banta,[2] next Cono, and Tene, all these lies eastward of the

Kingdom of Sherbro and well inhabated, but by reason of thier barborous custums its not safe to go among them. They say there's another nation to the eastward of all these inhabated by women only,[1] who at set times comes in the way of men in order to propagate thier specis and so returns. After this nation of the women the land is covered over with woods and unpassable mountains and marches, likewise large freshwater leakes. This is the country travilers[2] discriptian, which we are obiged to take here but not as to assert it for fact; and I see nothing very unlikely, as these people generley agree in the above discriptian without any other alteration. The Bulums go up once a year among these nations to trade for slaves and teeth and camwood[2] and other comodities, which is bought at easey rates in these wild nations, who are strangeers to the manafactories of Urope. A slave, as they say, is rated at 20 country bars, which when brought down here we buy for 45 or 50 bars and again sould on board a ship produces* 80 ships bars, which is above a 100 country bars or crowns, a considerable profit if other expences did not carry it away again, as I have said before in the first part of my Journal.

These people have a surprizeing manner of trying criminals in this part of the world, not much unlike the ancient Brittans in former ages, as follows.[3] If a person is suspected of any perticular crime and for

* In the year 1755.

54

want of evedence can't condem him by law, he is
taken by all his neibours and set upon a scaffold made
on perpose. In the main time there is a large quantity
of liquer prepar'd by a set person denominated by the
rest of the gang, of a strong poyson ; the offender is
obliged to drink a certain quantity of this liquer, which
if inocent they imagine it will have no power on him,
otherwise it kills him ; sometimes indeed they make
it stronger or weaker as they have a mind to favour
the person that drinks. This liquer is called " red
water " by the English, but the natives *Con* or *Kun.* I
have seen 2 or 3 instances of this false trials in this
country. As the above is fasse they have others that
brings things to light, which no power upon earth
could do without a devil or spirit. I have been a
witness of this myself, therefore I am the better able
to assert it, as follows : in York Island Sepmr. 21,
1756, there was a certain person on the island who at
several times had lost things of considerable worth,
without being able to find the person that stole the
above goods ; whereupon she made complaint to her
father in order to have his advice, who advized her to
send for a Mandinga priest,[1] who would soon discover
the person if he was on the island or to the fore at
the ceremoney. This was concluded and a man was
sent to call the priest, with out understanding upon
what acoumpt untill the minuet he landed, when all
the people in the town was gatherd togather, where
the person who lost the things told him her misfortune.

55

He answerd that if the offender was there he would soon discover him, which he did in the following manner. He ordred us all to sit down under a large orange tree and after he had placed himself in the midst, he drew forth an instrument, which you see [plate ix]. This instrument consisted of several joynts of cane wrought in dimonds, which upon the rizeing of his hand would gather it self up into his hand, likewise upon lowering his hand it would extend it self 3 or 4 feet long, and still in motion. This he held in his hand when any that was was demanded set down oposate the instrument, where if that person was ignorant of the theft it would retire to its master and lie close. We tried several in this maner but it gave no sighns of the thief untill an old woman was call'd, where upon it extended it self quite over to her breast, where it stood a while untill such time as the priest passed sentance on her as guiltey, where she conferm'd all by a confesion of the whole affair. This did not satisfy some preasent, who retired out of the place and takeing a small stone in one hand well hid and a stick in the other, demanded which hand the stone was in, whereupon it jumpt to the stone hand and so remaind untill it was open'd ; of this last trial we made several times which all fell out right. This made me imagine that they have some demon or evil spirit to guide them in these trials, as they are an ignorant people and unaquainted with slight of hand or other devices to blindfould the eyes of men. This priest was a Mahomitan of the Mandinga[1] nation, a people that has spread them selves all over these western parts of Africa and much esteem'd for thier holy lifes by the Bulums, notwithstanding they'll never take thier example. These people or Mandingas follows the laws of Mahomit according to the alchorn,[2] as they are lerned from the Moors in Barbary and elsewhere and so fetches it down here by these wandering pilgrims, who for thier holyness is suffer'd to pass and repass, where others would not. The Mindingoes are well skill'd in the Arabac tongues and writeings, begining where we end our lines in thier way of writeing; they write with a reed and use ink of a brown colour much the same as soot in England. They drink no strong liquer and are moderate in thier diet. They are an inland nation and very powerfull, these that live here are only kind of pilgrims, that has no place of ressedence but roves about among the Bulums as serves thier ends.

I shall now give a short discriptian of York Island in the river Sherbro, a place where our master chose for his houce and family. York Island is situated about 20 miles up the river and lies low, being mostly marchey ground and produces very little of any thing that might be serviceable to a family. Yet it is a pleasent place and covered over with palm trees. There stands on the N.E. side the rewins of an ancient castle, which was built by the English in former eages and abondon'd by them again, upon acount of

57

the decay of trade as we learn from the natives; there remains yet a small magazine and store house almost entire, with 2 small platforms for guns, as in the figr.[1]; it['s] surounded with a wall 5 or 6 feet high, likewise the tombs of some of the people that inhabatad in them times. This isle is reckn'd to be very unhelthey for white people, but as it is in the center of trade, it's commonly the ressedence of some white trader or other that perfers worldly riches before a heal constetution. We have built a house within the walls of the fort and clear'd away all the rubish.

June 20th   I have found the affects of this unhealthey air alreadey in this isle by pains in my bones and other simtoms of a bat health and but small incouragement in the way of trade this month; and the next is generly the worst in the year as to rain and hard gusts of wind.

July 15th   I receved the following letter from my brother, who is up the river a tradeing with 3 or 400 bars for slaves, which I insert as being mitteral to his removeal in order to mend his health something nearer the sea, his being then 40 miles from the mouth of the river at a place called Deong.[2]

" Deong July 12 1755,

I rece'd by the man Fonga 4 brass pans and 2 half pieces of baft and I am here almost alone, haveing no other company then Peter and my lanlord's woman. I have bought one pawn from Babong, so that I am quite out of sortments on acount of lending money to

58

Bereyboso for 2 slaves. I have sent the invoice of what good I have left, so that you may know how to assort me again.—Since I left you I have laboured under a phllgmalick maloncoly disposition of mind and no especely as I am in a sollitude not disagreeable to me and I have the more liberty to medatate and am also more adictted. Notwithstanding I endavour as much as possable to make my self contented in whatsoever state of life it may please providence to bring me. From your affte.

BLAYNEY OWEN."

As soon as I had receved this I went up the river to see him and sent him down to these parts and took his place where I made some remarks conserning Diong river.

From York island Deong bears east and after winding into several creeks and bays, begins to grow shoul at Berebosas' town, haveing many small towns upon its banks on both sides. This river by the country people's acount comes from an inland province called Goldfa,[2] where most of our camwood comes from. This town that goes by the name of Berebosa town takes its name from Berebosa, a black trader who lives there. The town consists of 7 houses built after the country fashion, as in [plate xi]. In this place I find several ugly things that's not common at York Island, such as long worms and *July 20th* 1755 frogs ; the later makes such horrid noises in the night that it breaks my sleep. Last night I found one of these worms under my bed

8 or 9 inches long, which was the ocasion of my not sleeping untill 11 or 12 a clook—as for snakes I have not found any since my arival, but my landlord informs me there are a great many a little way from the town.

This is certainly a very pleasnt place and very quiet, for when the natives call here they seldom make long ſtay, so that your trade's soon done. The house that's mark'd " c " is where I had my goods, " a " the port and " B " a canow lying at it.

As my manner of life may seem ſtrange to people of Europe I shall give a breef discription of my beſt liveing on the coaſt of Africa, as follows. When I am in the shalop¹ I seldom lie below ; if the weather's dry always upon a mat of the country make, as you see [plate ix., no. 1], covering myself with a cotten cloath and so sleep till morning. I haven't ocation for any other bed cloaths in the dry times. My diet is rice and fouls, sometimes salt provisions, palm oil and slabar sauce² of the country produce. When it can be had I use coffie, tea and chocolate, for we are seldom so happy as to have plentey of English provisions in this place. I live here, but not with so much ſtrength as I was want in Europe or any could climate ; my bones seems weaker and in hot weather I am favourish ; what moſt troubles is the musquetos, who hinders me from sleep at night, and in the day time large flyes supplys thier places, no less troublesom ; the bite of one of these flyes is so penetrateing that your shirt will hardly keep it out ; the pain is worse

PLATE XI

PART OF DEONG RIVER

[face p. 59

after the bites then for the present. To prevent these and other inconvenances the natives make laffers[1] for covering a dish of very curious workmanship, chiefly composed of the skin and branches of the she palm tree [as in plate ix., no. 3). Whenever they dress victuals, it's cover'd with one of these tolerable clean, a mat to sit down upon, for tables is useless among these people, but as the Moors of Barbary they eat upon the ground; this is all thier ambition in thier own houses. As thier diet is easey dreſt, so is thier apatite soon satisfy'd. Sometimes I have a large covering of callico made in the form of a house to keep of the flys at night, which ſtops thier enterance a little and in the morning take it down again. This is when I am up the rivers tradeing. I seldom take the trouble on board our shallop, as she is continualy moveing from one place to another in order to purchace the commodities that the country affords. Certainly a man in this country, especelly a Europeain, can have but little pleasure of his life, when he considers what it is to live in England, the hapyness of conversation, the pleasures of a life free from all these inconvenances which muſt certainly happen in this wilderness, where the inhabatents are hardly above beaſts, ignorant of all arts and siances, without the comforts of religion or the benefits that an engenous mind or person could shew them, without induſtery of cultavateing or manageing thier land to its perfection, deſtatute of all wholsom laws and paſt perswasion to enter into the civel society with the rest of mankind.

It may be imagined that white men on this coast live an uneasey life considering the aforesaid charectar of thes natives. To keep as far from these people as we can, we seldom get so far engaged with any black as to envolve ourselves into quarels, always sideing with the great men of the country who defends in case of quarels or any disturbance. I have always found that the country people are in dread of a white man. I have never yet been hurt by any in the towns where I have been tradeing, indeed they have stole all they could come at of my goods, such as knives, beads, and tabaco and such things as are handey to cary away, but never broak into my house to do me damage by confisticateing my goods. I have found them several times saucey and give bad langauge, but these afronts must be past, as you consider your self at thier mercy without the help of justice, you are liable to all thier abuses without means of revenge.

This makes [me] very often reflect on my situation, but when I consider my affears I am tyed to Africa; when I look back and servay what pleasures I'm obliged to shun by this retirement, I conclude myself so long out of the world, the flower of my age spent in obscuritey, and my mind is stall'd with the various prospects that has shew'd themselves to me alreadey in the course of my travils, that I can safely say I have sufficient, especaly in these parts. I am at a stand wheather or no to enlarge my work by travils ; and as I have great reason to shew my utmuſt thanks to the Disposeer of all things, Wo has carefully convay'd me through all the uncertainties of this life, ſtill to try my fortune again upon that angery element where I have been so often tosſt in war and pace. But as it has no respeƈt to persons therefore I reſt content, seeing a prince may endure is [*sic*] much or rather more then a common jack tar. It's to be considered that in the life of a saylor there is some things to sweetin the hardship of a voyage, as the hopes of seeing ſtrange countrys, the expeƈtation of gain and laſtly the joy of seeing your native country at your return ; indeed saylors are commonly mery, hartey people and wares out the difficultey of a voyage with patience, but upon thier return lay out the fruts of thier labour in debaucherys, without consideration of future wants. This I always found to be the charetar of an English seaman in my long experance upon that element of 8 or 9 years, in which time I have had very little communication with my country or any place else, except the time of loading and dischargeing our ship in whatever place we ware consighn'd. I muſt say the life of a seaman is is no ways agreeable to a man of quiet disposition, but he that is wild and rakeeshly inclin'd, turbilant in his manners and loves liquer and bad company, shall very often have the uper hand in a ship's crew. This is in a general way, some indeed there are that is of a diffrt. chareƈter as light is from

63

darkness. I am not giveing this charectar to every one of that proffes'n, only to these common people who is strangers to edication or good breeding There's a dail to be said conserning the management of oficers, who under [a] quet captain to shew thier athoritey use the people without mercy in these several ways :—first, in stinting them of thier victuals, secondly in keeping them to stricter disapline then is necessary for the preservation of ship and men, with ordering things that is not needfull, upon no other acount then to keep the people at work. But to conclude I think in my opinion that a saylor that has no other means to satisfy the nececereys of this life then sailing the sais for wages, I look upon him to be more miserable then a poor farmer who lives upon his labour, who can rest at night upon a bed of straw in obscurity, then a saylor who comforts him self in the main top by blowing of his fingers in a frostey night.

August 9th
1755

The rest of this month there has hapn'd nothing perticular only our sailing down to the island Plantains for a supply of goods and our return again up the river Sherbrow. And this year hapen'd as quarel between a certain gentelman who lives on the island Plantains and Mr. Hall, our master, as follows. This gentelman had a black servant that was under condemnation of drinking red water or poyson for a crime that's hardly worthey of inserting, at the same time we lay there with the

August 20
1756 [sic][1]

64

shalop; this fellow makes his escape at night and swam on board our vessell. There being no watch held that night gave him an opertunity of sliping a canno away from our ſtern and so escaped home to his frinds in the country. When this came to be known in the morning, one of our people was secur'd in his place and we ware accused of procureing his escape. As our man was a free man it would be a dangerous consequence to suffer him to lie in confinement, therefore Mr. Hall returnd to Sherbro and laid the case before the King, who told him that he muſt ingage a lawsute with Mr. * and his people and to secure the firſt that came in his way of that partey, moreover told him he would ſtand his friend in every shape as far as lay in his power. With this incouragement Mr. * canou was ſtopt upon her passage up the river and 5 people put in irons upon the above acount, the affeɕt of which brought Mr. * up in his shallop in order to have it tryd by country law. In the main time the King of Sherbro broke of from Mr. Hall, and like a true black torned tail to our side and assiſted the oposate partey, and after great expence on both sides it was agreed that Mr. Hall should deliver up his prisoners and receve his single man, which was the end of this unhapy affair. The expences in this afair on both sides could not be less than 300 bars, notwithſtanding Mr. Hall was censured by all white people as a piece of engratitude, as he lay under a great many obligations to Mr. *. This affair was the chief occation of Mr. Hall's intention of laveing the coaſt of Africa. In the maintime I reflected on the unhappy ſtate of man that truſts to false friends either black or white and is a good inſtance to mintain my charactar of the negroes on the coaſt, as it's plainly seen that notwithſtanding this man was the father or king of so many people yet could not in one article keep up to the rules [of] juſtice or friendship, but basely betray the man who put his trust in him and for the sake of a little gain lay him open to all his enemies to ſtand or fall.

Sepmr. Some men pine at what they think misfortunes, for there are a great many, indeed moſt people, does not know what is a misfortune, or to diſtinguish between a good or bad fortune. It's not what you desire that you should call a good fortune, for the desires of man are vain ; therefore what may happen to your dislike for the present may hereafter turn to your advantage, as He that rules all things lays it out to the beſt advantage for His creatures. Therefore it's presumtion in a man to lay any blame to fortune because the common axcedents of life dos not fall out to his likeing, so as this gentelman, as I have spoken of before in the begining of my Journal, mintain'd this opinion in all the parts of his life. It was a great misfortune that would change his humour in any respect, he was always generous in the loweſt of his circumſtances, never careing for riches but as it was supservant to his pleasures, seldom out of humour

66

and gay in his cloathing even among negroes, not-withstanding he held corispondance with the greatest traders in Africa and Europe, who used the slave trade untill his departure for the West Indies with Capt. Easton of New London, who recev'd him on board 1756.

As there is nothing extrornery in my Journal of this month I shall fill up with some remarks on my new capt. and ship. It very often happens in New England that if a man is esteem'd for his honstey in publick, let him be of what profession so ever, he is to be prefer'd in a ship to these and other parts of the world, if he can take an observation and is acquainted with that part of navagation call'd plain sailing, without any of the practical part of seamanship. So that it's nothing strange to see a butcher, carpinter, or farmer, master of one these vessells, notwithstanding they sometimes make good voyages and returns safe home more by chance then art. There's a great many remarks of simplisity laid to the charge of these people by Europains, which I find no reason why they should not be commended rather then a matter of laughter, as they supply the places of swearing and imprecations, which our old Europains are two much in love with ; however, all that can be laid to their charge can never dominish thier well known charectar of an industurious honest people, who dispizes the gaudey toys of the foolish for things more substansial and nececary for the life of man.

In America there's great differances in religion, first
the High Church, Low Church, Quaqers, New
Lights,[1] Old Lights, Ana-baptists. Notwithstanding
these sects there's very little disturbance conserning
religion on any side, every man going where his
incliineation leades him, save the Roman Catholick,
who is utterly denied the publick use of his profession
in almost all parts of America except Maryland, where
they are tolerated to build chappels all over that
province. Capt. Easton was one of these men that
for want of good breeding was obliged to keep himself
in countinance among company by being always in
haste, especealy when there was any part of discourse
brought in that did not consern farming or common
busnes, as selling or buying of slaves, which he was
very good at. It may seem something creuil to
expose a man's charectar as above, without some reason
or other to iustiefy so henious a proceeding as follows.
It was common after company was broke up and every
man at quarters, that Capt. Easton began his discourse
conserning the absent company in the most ungenerous
terms, as how Mr. Such-a-one was deeply indepted, or
another's wife was under suspision of takeing an
opertunity while her husband was tradeing in the
country, occasiond him to be noted amongst all his
aquainatance in Africa. He had good oficers and
commonly made good voyages for his merchants,
which might be the occasion of his perferment at
home.

68

Untill the 7th there has hapn'd nothing
March 1st
1756
remarkable or any news from the southward. The 8th Capt. Godfrey arived in
Sieralone and gave us a full discriptian of Crown
Point engagement[1] between the Frinch and English
in North America. The rest of this month has has
been spent in tradeing for slaves without any thing
remarkable.

The 1, 2, 3d I saild up* Denbey river[2] in
April 1st
Capt. Easton's boat, almoast to its rize at
a place called Mongey Sebos town. This river is
very long and navagable to the foresaid town, full of
alegators as almost all the rivers in the Susses[3] are.
The people in these parts differs very much from the
nation of the Bulums. They have no Kings or *Pora
men* whereby they can extort money from you ; the
most part of your trade is left to your lanlord, who
expects 3 bars for every slave that he purchaceses, so
that your trouble's but small in tradeing here.

Receved advice from† Bassow,[4] that part
Aprill 3rd
of the city of Lisbon is distroy'd by an
earthquake,[5] and the remaining part considerabley
damaged by certain Spaniards who made use of that
unhappy juncture to plunder the town, the royal
familey escapeing without hurt into the ajoyning
country. This news came by a canow from Bassow,
likewise informed us that there was 2 Brazile ships to

* a river in the Susser on the north Coast of Africa.
† a Portague factory to the Northward.

69

the N'ward tradeing for slaves. This canno came down in order to purchace cole, or cola, a fruit that's esteem'd very much at Gambia and Catchew and serves for part of thier asortments in theer country trade for slaves and teeth ; it's purch'd here at easey rates—the fruit consists of 5 or 6 kernils in one cod and groes sometimes as big as a man's fist ; its a good bitter and relishes water.

Sepmr 21 Untill September there has nothing happen'd of consequence. Set sail for Sieralone and arived there the 24th, a 60 gun ship lyeing there the same time, a great quarrel between the capt. and the black people a shoar, which was the ocasion of 5 men being kil'd on the black people's side.

Sepmr 25 Arived at York Island. October, Novembr. and Decmr. has pass'd without any thing remarkable. January and Febery we have concluded to lave York Island and remove more to the Southw'd under the protection of a malato who bears great sway in the country. In this place we have erected a house upon the bank of the river and even here we are subject to pilavers and lawsuits, all owing to the people we are obliged to keep in our own house. This is the first of our tradeing upon our own acoumpts, this being our summer season. These 2 months past we have had several engagements between the Frinch and English, the Liverpool men has had the loss of 6 or 8 of thier ships in the enterprize ; this has taken up untill Aprill without any thing else of note or moment.

May 1
1757

It seems to mee that the blacks on this coast retains their ancient custums without alteration in any thing, except thier cloathing, which alters a good dail by the help of Europain cloath, swords, and household furneture, likewise has made some adition to thier granduer with our goods in general. As to our religon it has made no impression in the least otherwise then a matter of redicule or laughter in so many years as they have had us among them, notwithstanding there has been some trials to convert them to a notion of a better state.

20th 1757

We have been surprized this morning with finding our store broaken open and tabaco, rum and other goods to the value of 10 or 12 crowns or bars caried away, and very little sighns of finding out the theves, otherwise then by the Mandingo envention menthon'd in the fore part of my Journal, which we intend to try out of curiousety at its wonderfull vertue as soon as the priest comes home. It's not reasonable that a Cristian should trust to or belive in these things, or belive that they are able to perform anything above the common sort of men, yet what a man sees before him, and by nothing but a little common sand, may find out the secrets of futurity, must be aledged to the power of some evil spirit or famileer, sent by that great enemy of mankind to draw these ignorant wretches to him self.

71

Saturdday May the 27th We have great reioyceing in the country upon the return of some free people from on board a ship commanded by Willm. Morgan from the Dainish West Indies who stopt these people on board his boat and put them in irons as slaves, takeing for thier ransom eight prime slaves before he agreed to thier discharge, against all law or reason.[1]

This month affords nothing extromery of mark or note, except on acount of the execution of Admiral Byng[2] for some misdemeanours up the Streights the last year and some small advantages that the French has had upon this coast. It has been seldom known such a scarcety of shiping upon this coast as at this pressent time and such a bad time of trade ; from Siera Lone to Cape Mount there [is] not above 3 or 4 sail of ships that come for trade, which is of bad consequence to us that lives in the country, depending upon quik returns of goods and the blacks keeping up to thier old price, let it be war or pace, besides the great expences of our houses and kings, which is not much less than 50 crowns pr. month, one month with another, which is a great expence. Lately there died a gentelman here that has spent 12 or 13 years in this country before he could aquire a fortune sufficent to live in Urope—he was a man that was adictted to great misfortunes, but bore up in all his afflictions with remarkable patience. He was called Thos. Lorimoor.

72

Now indeed I have some respite from busness and the hurry of the world. This place is free from the common people that used to flock to us at York Island, which was the occation of a great many disturbances that we are now free from, and yet we are not destatute of trade, as we have bought 3 slaves and 2 teeth besides screvelas[1] in the space of 2 months, without looking looking [*sic*] for it. As I am much inclin'd to be malloncoly, this place so far suits with my inclineations that if it ware not for sertain domestic troubles I should think my self happy even in this miserable country, without ever thinking of Europe or its pleasures. From my window I can see all the jiascent country with part of the River Sherbro and the King's town to the east, again to the west the sea lies open to your view, with the dreadfull waves that rools over the barr and shouls in the the mouth of the river, which occations a murmuring noise even at the house where we live. As this month is the time for planting all kinds vigetables, I imploy some of my time in sowing and planting watermelons, pompions,[2] guinea peas,[3] and other things that's necescery for our houshould use. This is my morning's work and as the sun rises I employ the people in hedgeing my several little gardins in, to keep out the crabs, snakes, or other vermin. This is the chief imployment of my more retired hours, when I think my self happy. By and by comes a great troop of canows full of negros with thier several commodites to sell, one fetches

73

kamwood, another fouls, a third a bunch of plantains
or sume rice, one complaining I have him no dram,
another says as much for tabaco and a third is hungary,
another beings his part for service* (as they term it)
for which I am obliged to return more then it's worth
at his departure, otherwise there's a pilavour. Now,
I say, begins my trouble and a frusteration of these few
minits I past before in agreeable quiet, comforting
my self that God will in his due time bring me among
Cristians and my native people, where I may perhaps
injoy the pleasures that I am so long absent from and
with joy call to mind the many changes of fortune that
Providence has safely convey'd me
June 7th through. 3 or 4 days since there has
1757 hapn'd a remarkable quarrel between 2
great men in the country where I live, and as nothing
escapes my journal of moment, I have inserted it as
follows. Some time sence there hapn'd a law suit
between Samankebora and Casive, the first master or
magestrate of the town of Mano, the other of the town
of Mania. This affair, as all others is in this country,
was to be decided by a jury of indifferant persons ; as
they ware disputeing in the house upon several heads,
they rose at last to high words and from that to bad
names, whereupon Samankebora drew his scymiter
and cut two of Casive's fingers of, against the laws of
the country. He was immedately secured and put in

* For service is when they come to see you with some small pressent
to make them welcom.

74

irons and condem'd to have all his substance confisti-
cated, his house burnt and himself obliged to drink
poyson, or have his hand cut of as the other, which
last is the most easey punishment. So regourous is
thier laws against drawing of blood in their *Pora* way
that none of the great men dare say any thing to soften
the punisment, without the offended will come to a
composition and then 4 or 5 slaves will hardly make it
up. The chief reason of this punishment was upon
Casive's calling them names names [*sic*] in the *Pora*
way to kill him and take his affects, which when once
they name the *Pora* they can't draw back, but is the
same as swearing on oth.

*June 13th
Munday* Last night the devil has been here makeing
his usual noise among the bushes about
Samankaboro's pilaver, as I have spoken
of before; it's not determind yet, either to kill
or save.

19th It's all decided and his life saved, with the
loss only of 5 slaves.

Capt. Whitson's arival at Serelone.

July has past without any thing meteral, saveing the
great decay of trade in these parts occasion'd by the
French war and scarcety of English shiping, which has
rendred the price of a slave 10 bars less then usual, so
that the common price abard a ship is 70 bars. I have
been lately at Sieralone with 4 slaves, but was obliged
to return 3, the captain was so nice; the amount of my
goods for one slave with teeth and wood was 140

75

ships bars, which we have traded upon untill August
5, and we are readey again for another
voyage to the same place with 5 slaves,
good and bad togather, for dry goods. As I have
nothing extrornery to fill up this part of
the month I shall make up that by giveing a charactar of a certain mallata man in
these parts, who has aquired a great fortune by his
skill and some other abillites in the way of trade.

Augst 1757

*Saturday
6th*

"He commonly goes by the name of Henry Tucker
and lives upon the same shoar as we do about a mile
distant. He has been in England, Spain and Portugall
and is master of the English tongue; he has 6 or 7
wives and a numerous ofspring of suns and daughters;
his strength consists of his own slaves and their
children, who has built a town about him and serves
as his gremetos upon all occassions. This man bears
the charectar of a fair trader among the Europeans,
but to the contrary among the blacks. His riches sets
him above the Kings and his numerous people above
being surprized by war; almost all the blacks ows him
money, which bring a dread of being stopt upon that
acount, so that he is esteem'd and feared by all who has
the misfortune to be in his power. He's a fat man and
fair spoken, and lives after the manner of the English,
haveing his house well furnish'd with English goods
and his table tolarably well furnish'd with the country
produce. He dresses gayley and commonly makes us of
silver at his table, haveing a good side board of plate."

August 16*th*
1757

I find that its with the greatest care and circumspection that we can keep things in any tolerable order as to the way of trade, but find our stock dominish rather then encrace, occasion'd by the war at home and the wakeness of trade here. It's terable to consider our situation. If we go home we are liable to be taken by the Frensh, if we remain here we are surounded by the worst of people, who considers nothing but the your [*sic*] abilites to do them service, when your money's gone so is thier friendship and assistance tow. We are here only 7 degrees from the line and above 2900 miles from our native seat, among a barbarous people that nous neither God or a good quality in man. Some people may think it strange that we should stay so long among people of the above charetar, when we have so many opertuniteys of going of the coast home. But I say, as Europe is certainly the garden of the world, yet there's very little groes there for a passing traveler for nothing. A man that has spent his prime abroad, notwithstanding all his misfortunes, as ship-wrecks, plundering, and and [*sic*] a hundred other things that ocors in the life of a saylor, I say that these things will not keep him from the charetar of a proddigal sun, who has spent his time idely abroad. And now he comes home as a useless burthen to his friends the first thing that you hear is your name spred all over the town as the greatest liar in the world, so that all you have to do is to hold your tongue and be

77

contented with the common name of " the Mallato
juſt come from Guinea." Otherwise if your pockets
is well ſtuf'd with gold, that very perticular hides all
other infirmities, then you have hapes of frinds of all
kinds thronging and wateing for your commands.
Then your known by the name of " the African
gentleman " at every great man's house, and your
discource is set down as perticular as Criſtopher
Culumbus's expedition in America. Any one that
makes any doupt is reckon'd an atheiſt and has a
desighn to afront you, notwithſtanding you[r] well
known chareɗar of a very injenious gentelman, who
has made so good use of his time as to provide for a
rainey day.

It's not every man's fortune to get money, tho' of
the greateſt capasity, yet them that's look't upon as
dull wretches as to other affairs commonly has the
greateſt bank. Let a man be ever so deligent and
have bad fortune, the commons of the world will
never belive otherwise then it's oueing to his extrava-
gences in some sort or other. This refleɗion brings
to my mind a certain person that I have sail'd with
from North America to these parts, who had sail'd
with the Lord Anson in almoſt all his undertakeings, in
the quality of a mate. This person had all the good
fortune that could be expeɗed and upon his return
home found himself worth 17 or 18 hundred pounds
ster. This money he laid out in America in part of
the purchace of a ship with 2 other gentelmen, in order

PLATE XII

A CAMELIAN FROM KING SUMANA

[face p. 79

to trade to other parts of the world.   These 3 disigreed apon some frivelous affair, which put a ſtop to the desighn ; carpinters, rigers, and sail-makers became troublesome, so that my frind was oblig'd to obscond, and was verry glad to find him self on board a sloop with me in the quallity of a comon sailor, where we sail'd to the coaſt of Africa and after an aquaintance [of] 14 or 15 weekes, could never find any thing to dominish his chareɛtar of an induſterous, pious, good man, who after all his grandour and and [*sic*] good fortune could bear that of adversity with a submisive patience and clear mind, which is sufficent to shew that riches is not aquired by deligency or management, but as lottery, some draws a prize and others a blank. Yet there may be a great dail in a carefull vigilantcy in inspeɛting into what ever comes to your lot of busness, and giving your self a method or rule for every per-ticular branch, letting nothing escape, of the smalleſt matter of advantage without a place in your care : this I say in time will augment the principle and is a sure way of going on, except as misfortune, as above, should demolish all and lave you to begin again, as my frind above, who has since died at the caſtle in Sieralone of a favoor.

I have lately been presented with a *Auguſt* 16*th* camelian[1] from King Sumana, which 1757 you see in full [plate xii.], exaɛtly as it apear'd to me.   I kept is [*sic*] 4 or 5 days, when it made its escape by biteing the thread that held its leg, in

79

the night.   The figr. above represents the creature
when its makeing a posture of defence
August 19*th*   against anything that offends it.   I have
57   try'd it several times as to its changeing
colour, and could never see it alter but to black
and deep yallow, except at night when it was sure to
sleep in a fine orange, altering its shape to a great
lenth.

This month brings in many alterations in our
circumstances, which for diffrt. ends we have agreed
to seperate ourselves about a mile distant from where
we lately settled, not in any anger or quarell but for
the convenancy of trade, in order to be sooner of the
coast among our own sort.

It's surprizing to consider the many turns of fortune
we have undergone in this heathen world,   the
calamities, the wrecks of our fortunes and minds, has
been enough to lay us in our graves, without the help
of patience and God's assistance, Who has miracllously
preserved us from the danger attending a seafareing
life.   August 20th 1757[1].   All people here is surprized
that the government has not sent out any of our men
of war upon these coasts in these troublesom times to
secure our marchant ships,[2] when in pace we are
sure to have 3 or 4 ships of force every year,[3] we
have lost lately 7 or 8 sail upon this coast and are
still in fear of more by the Frinch priviteers and
ships of war, so that its hardly safe to venture out in
boats.

80

August 22*d* I have seen another surprizeing trial of the Mandingo witchcraft here, upon occasion of ſtolen goods, which goes beand all dispute as to its suretey—this man not only told the theef, but perform'd other things of miriclous nature. After he had told all conserning the goods he ordred a bason to be fill'd full of nuts, which was brought, then desired us to chuse out any one in his absence and mix it with the reſt, and upon his return he shew'd us our nut after makeing some prayers—this was done several times. There is nothing but this man can tell with the greateſt ease—if your boat be abroad he tells you every little triffleing axcedent that hapn'd in the passage and you may expeᴄt thier ſtay so long or so short. It put me in mind of the laſt trip that Mr. Tucker's schooner left this, bound for Sieralone. 2 days after we ware discourseing conserning the vessell, the old man reply'd that the scooner would be here today at an anchor, which set us all a laughing, and several of us told him that his conjuouration was false. However before night the vessell arived, haveing met a vessell from England at the Plantains, which was the occasion of her quick return.

It[1] was of a brown colour, enclineing to a sky bleu towards the head, and after we had kill'd it there remain'd a noiceous sent in the house. As there's nothing more offencive to me then any of that kind, I can hardly sleep at night for thinking that there may be another about my bed or under the mats of my room,

81

6

which is the occasion that I keep great fires all night in hopes that the smoak will banish these dangerous creatures from my habbitation.

Septmr 16th I have just arived from Sieralone, after selling 18 quental of camwood and a slave, and brought home 160 ships bars, the whole amount of my pressent stock in dry goods, and now my brother has gone the same voyage with the same kind of cargo—same time 2 men of war[1] lyeing there and readey to sail for the Gold Coast.

Sepmr 24 I have laid out all my cargo alreadey in camwood and a slave, and find that I have augmented my cargo 63 bars since my last.

Octobr 11th This is my second arival from Sieralone where I receved news from England that the Duke of Comberland is defated by the French and likewise the King of Prusia.[2]

There has been a terable instance of lightning at Siralon while I was there. In the midst of a turnado a flash of lightning struck a briganteen and not only disabled her masts but kill'd 2 men upon deck and disabled a third terably.

Octobr 19th *1757* We have had terable news this last week from Sieralone of the want of supplys from England of tradeing goods, so that they have left of buying slaves from white traders. Few or no shiping has been here this 2 months. We have no other news from England since my last voyage to Sieralone then the late battles in Germany.

82

October 30th

Sunday

Monday

I have given a discriptian in the begining of my Journal of the island of Fogo, and now by Capt. Pintar, we have the news that the island has suffered very much by an earthquak, so that the fire is totaley extingush'd and considerable damage done to the inhabatants, haveing the pike or volcano wholely caried away. It was acompaney'd with hurrycanes and terable gusts of wind. It hapned at midnight, so that by the light of the afforesaid volcano that every thing apeared plain as day at the island of Brava, which is 8 or 9 leagues distant.

It is surprizeing to consider the callamitey of the Portaguse in differant parts of the world this year : the dreadfull affair of Lisbon,[1] the Western Isles and now Fogo are instances that has not been in many ageas seen. It is further observed by my author that after the earthquake happn'd in Fogo several springs of fresh watter stopt and became wholely dry on the island St. Jago, which is 5 or 6 leagues distant, and the sea between the 2 islands of a wonderous depth.

Novmr 7th 1757

Yesterday there apeared a long boat close to the shoar of our point standing out to sea—all that we could do could not bring her tow or spake her. The same day Mr. Tucker's boat went over the bar in order to proceed her voyage to Cape Mount.

Some days ago I set of in order to go to Cape Mount to sell my slaves which amounted to only 2

prime men.   These I caried down to the Turtle
Islands in order to pass the bar, which I

did and in my pasage I spoke a ship from
Liverpool, Capt. Sodtherd, about 3 hun-
dred tuns, Frinch built and lately taken from that nation
by a small privitteer belonging to Liverpool.   With
this ship I traded and brought home 140 ships bars
without any other remarkable axcedent in my voyage.

22d

3 or 4 days past there has been a great
take of manatee¹ or sea cow in our river,
a creature of a very ugly form but good eateing, about
the size of a cow but rather resembles hog in all but
its tail and its want of feet.   It's monsterous fat,
haveing a skin an inch thick.

28th

There has been a most barbarous instance
of the creuel nature of these wretched
people nigh where I live 2 days ago.   It's the method
of these me[n] that I am going to spake of to dress
themselves up in the bark of a tree untill they resemble
an alegator, then they lurk in secret places to surprize
any inocent person that has the fortune to pass that
way in the night.   As soon as thier prize is secure,
they devour him² without mercey along with thier
ascociates in the bushes, who has prapared a fire for
that purpose.   The other night a yong man was stopt
in his cano by one of these Hottentots as [he] lay
fishing in the river and with the greatest difficulty
escaped to a nabouring town on the river side, where
he was a considerable time before he came to himself

PLATE XIII

The RIVER SHARBOW

OWEN'S HOUSE ON THE SHERBRO

[face p. 85

again. Thier laws allows immadate death to the person that's convicted of this crime by drinking red water, and thier bodies burnt to ashes.

Sunday 30th Since me and my brother's seperation into diffrt. houses I thing our affairs turns out better then we expected, both for his good and mine as to circumstances. His house is finish'd by the assistance of our good frind Mr. Tucker with very little expence to the owner. As our houses are not built for durance or strength, we can soon erect one of long sticks muded over and whitewash'd, haveing the inside lineed with mats and well thatched aloft. I have drawn an exact draft of mine [plate xiii.] as it now stands, with part of the river runing before it. About 20 yards from my house stands that of my people, likewise my cookroom under the letter B backwards. In this retreat I live a very remarkabl life and if it wasn't for my woman, and 4 or 5 people I miyht very well pass for an hermit. My diet is main, and my cloathing not sumtious. If any of the blacks comes I buy their commoditeys at as cheap a rate as I can, which enables me to trade a board the ships once or twice pr. month, which just keeps me from sinking in the principle stock. Some people may condem this kind of life, and perferr that of a venturious sailor or valliant soldier, but I can tell them to try both first and then take thier choice. One of these lives I have tried 8 or 9 years both in pace and war, and found nothing to intice a man of a good

85

disposition to a continuance in an imployment wherein vice and ignorance bare the garland garland [*sic*] from virtue and honour.

These people who generly are from a poor stock, when they find them selves growing by degrees a little above thier useal latd. in the circumstances of life, dispise all these men that begun upon the same footing, but perhaps had not the same good fortune to atain to any pitch in worldly grandour, as for instance lately among us here, where there's so few one wod think that they wod not fall out or show a bad example to the natives, as follows. For several years past this coast has been frequented by 2 captns. from diffrt. parts of the world, both English by birth. These men held a very great corispondance with each other for severl years in point of friendship, untill this last year, where they hapned to [be] bound to differnt parts of the coast. Capt. P. B. went to Gambia in order to trade, the other, whoom I distinguish by the letters C.P., tradeed here, where he acording to custum landed his good and made a store in order to make quicker dispth. off the coast. This store happn'd to be burnt by axcedent, where besides his goods hee lost the ship's papers and others of value. Notwithstanding he with the rest of his cargo set sail for Gambia, where he expected that his old frind Capt. P.B. would help him what lay in his power to make up his loss. Upon his arival he was receved with all marks of respect by his old frind; they drank and eat togather and parted for the first night. In the morning Capt. P.B. returned his vissit and in his company 7 or 8 soldiers from the fort in order to saze Capt. C.P., ship and slaves by reason he had no papers on board. The poor man made all the deffence he could, but all to no porpose ; he was sazed and is now tradeing among us here in a long boat, reflecting on that unnatureall villan who sacrafised his honour, friendship and all for the sake of ill got riches. You'll hardly meet with such an action of villany in these natives towards one and other. I have heard since that Capt. C.P.'s letters has got home, where he has aleged that his papers ware burnt by axcedents and that he has a cirtifficate of his his [*sic*] misfortunes from most of the white traders on the coast, so that the Commons[1] has taken it in to consideration to persiqut Cap. P.B. at law as soon as his arival.

Decmr 1   There's news just arived from the inland kingdoms that the locusts are come down among them, which gives us great reason to expect them here, to the utter distruction of our rice and other grain.

Janr   I herd a sloop arived here from Gambia, John Engledue commander, for camwood. The times is so extrornery bad that he has brought the price from 6 bars to 4 for wood and has landed his cargo in order to purchace 20 tuns at the above price, to the determent of us traders. The shiping is still growing scarscer, so that it's the opinion of several that the whites will be obliged to go home if the war

87

continues any considerable time. As for my self I
live in the ſtation of a hermit and make my self contented with my preſſent circumſtances since I find it
impoſſable to go of without a dail of danger danger
[*sic*] and risque. Yet it's a dail of comfort to me

Janur 5
1757-8

that I can sit down in my own cabbin,
after all my ſufferings and hardships and
injoy the fruts of a quiet retirement,
which is a ſerenety of mind that a man can seldom
attain to when he mixes with the busey part of mankind. I look upon the reſt of the world as a scene of
trouble and vanity. Europe, that ought to be the seet of
all happyness that this life can afford, is now invoul'd
in bloodey wars and all other calamiteys atending
it—here I sit down and refleċt upon both without
any danger from either, excep the want of goods.
Not but that I wod ſuffer a great dail to do my country
service in any quality so ever, but fortune has disposed
of me otherwise, and I muſt be contented with my
lot without complaining. These refleċtions I confess
sometimes eases my mind from a desire of returning
to my native country. With these and other remarks
I fill up a leaf when I want other matter from the
produċt of the country. I shall conclude this with
with a discriptian of a certain creature that I found
ajouning to my house, which I think to be very
surprizeing in its kind. I have shown it [plate
xiv.] in the position that it commonly lies when
it's feeding. It's called by the natives *Zeatabongia*

88

PLATE XIV

(A) A CROCODILE

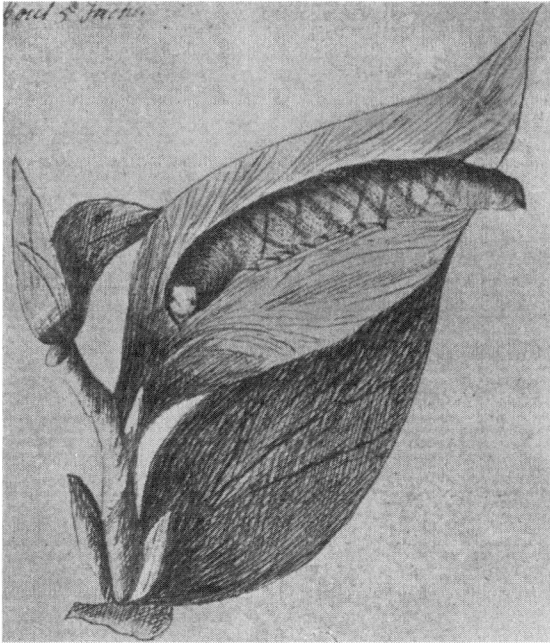

A ZEATABONGIA, A YELLOW WORM

It is likewise observed of this creature that if you tramp upon it unawares,
so that any of its blood tutches your flesh the part affected swells very much
and is in danger of mortifycation

[*face p.* 89

or the yellow worm,[1] it's seldom seen in the rains. The natives say that this creature is very dangerous in case you stoop to observe it more plain then at a distance, it will rise of the ground with a very swift motion and grasp any part of your face that fasten on, with great pain to the person and can never be seperated without cutting in pieces. I caught 4 of them this evening upon a small bush adjoyning to my house. It's about 5 inches long and of a gold colour, armed with sharp claws risembleing these of a cat, and seems a dull sloathfull creature, not at all agreeing with the discriptian the blacks gives it as to its motion.

I have likewise observed that it's verry quick in distroying the bush that it feedes on, haveing eat up a whole shrub in 24 hours to the stem.

Janury 10*th*
1757-8

Capt. Engledue upon his comeing up the river refus'd the King his custum, which has bred a great pilaver between the King and all the whites, so that it's dangerous to pass or repass in the river. It has cost Mr. Tucker 4 or 5 bars and is not finished yet. 2 or 3 days ago we have had Capt. Gauthers from Liverpool, one of the ships that was taken by the Frinch last year.

Janry 12

There has an axcedent hapn'd in my familey that I can't help seting down for its sinlelarity as follows. Last month I sent my people in the country to purchace a slave and my head man in his voage was taken with the small pox. As soon as he found him self better he sent for a conjour or

Mandingo in order to find out the person who struck
him with this distemper, for the blacks never think
that any sickness comes but by a witch or divil. The
Mindingo was call'd and after all ceremonies was over
he told the man that in my house there was 2 yong
girls and one of them was the instrument of convaying
his sickness to him by witchcraft, whereupon he sent
3 of my people down to me for a supply of goods.
Wn. they told me what the man said I call'd the girls
and one of them confesst the whole, that she had
receved something from a sertan person to throw at
the man, according to the Mindingo ['s] words, which
is without doupt a sure proof of these people's
deailing with the devile. There's a great many whites
that thinks all these thing are false, but what a man
sees and imploys his reason upon upon [*sic*] must have
some grounds of truth. Neither do I think it any way
unlikely, since we have examples in all ages of the
power of witchcraft among persons who dedicate
themselves to that impious practice ; every day I see
examples of this kind where I live. I shall fill up this
day's work with an affair that hapn'd between Mr.
Tucker and his eldest brother Peter. These 2 men
has lived about 30 or 40 years in this part of Africa ;
the elder is under many obligations to the yonger
these many years, as to lending of money and helping
him to all the necessarys of his house, cloathing his
children and other smaller favoors, which is requited
in the following barbarous manner. 4 or 5 years

ago he was found in a conspirey against his life for the sake of his riches and now he is found in another, wherein he has sided with the kings, or rather prompted them to stop his boats, to take goods out by force under a colour of duty, to make his inocent brother as poor as himself and yet he has the face still to apear in his brother's pressence.

13   I have been on board of Capt. Engledo today, where I found him employ'd in makeing a curious piece of shell work in his cabbin upon an old picture. Tomorrow I entend to imatate him as nigh as my abilites will alow, as we have great numbers of shells upon the beetch.

Friday 14   I have just finish'd my shell work and I think it's just shuteable to my dwelling. It's of a round form with a looking glass in the midle; I have wrought it into divers figures with various kinds of shell and moss taken from the bark of old trees and shrubs, which I have laid on with turpintine and bees wax boiled well together into a hard substance. I find myself at a great loss for want of Indian ink for drawing my drafts in my Journal. I am forced to use a pen in its sted, which is the occasion of my laveing out severall drafts for want of the above necessary. With these and others of the same nature of amusements I pass the tedeus hours of my life away, not without hope still that I shall once more be better acommadated in a Cristian country, after these broils is ended that detains me here in Africa.

17th Sunday We have had the news of the death of the King of Sheffra yesterday, who was poyson'd in the following manner. Some time ago he and another great man went to sacrifice to his gregory or witch, but in his path was surprized by a snake, so that they ware obliged to return and regale themselves over a pot of wine, which lull'd them to sleep. The other in the morning was found dead in his bed and the King was taken with great pains, so that all one side of his bodey is dead and 2 days ago was just able to spake, when he made the following confession. He said that he had poisoned 2 of his brothers formerly and at other times 5 of his people, and that his pressent illness was a judgement of God for his wickedness to his brothers and others—a dreadfull thing to die with a bad consience.

Friday 9th 2 days ago one of my people kill'd a large sawfish close to the point where we live; its saw measured 3 feet and about 4 inches broad. Nothing else of moment.

Saturday The King of Sheffora is now dead and they have crown'd a new king, but I can't tell wheather he is of any affinity to the disseas'd king, who has had a reighn or 8 or 9 years—all the kings round about is summon'd at the sollomnty and old Sheffra is forgot for ever.

Saturday There is a very great king come down from the inland kingdoms. A caries, all by conquest and the laws of arms. He has made 2 or 3

PLATE XV

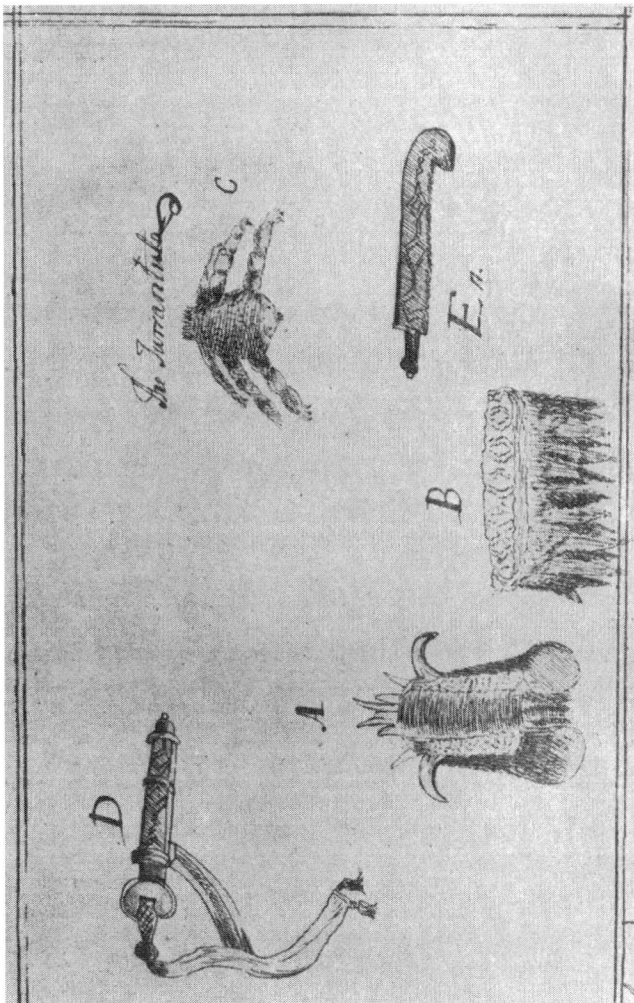

ELEPHANT'S GRINDERS. A TARANTELLA. AND A SCIMITAR

[face p. 93

pety kingdoms subject to him aready. My self has bought several of his slaves and he cuts towe great a figure to be forgotten. He's a Manding and goes by the name of King Furry Do.[1] He's a great dread to all the kings up in the country, who lyes near his incroahments.

March 16th 1758 2 months has run on without any thing pirticular except the circumstances of the English war and the arival of Capt. Taylor from London, who has brought supplys of the castle at Sieralone.

Friday 17th This morning my people killed a very large spider[2] in the cookroom, all covered over with long hair and verry dreadful to look at. Its bite is esteemed as bad as that of a snake, its legs are as thick as the small end of a tabaco pipe and set full of bags or places in the skin fill'd with blew liquer, as it is seen transperant through the skin, it feet are armed with claws mixed with hair of a brown colour. I k[n]ow of nothing is [*sic*] resembles so much as a sea crab.

I have lately arived from the Plantains where I saw a sea horse's under-jaw brought ashoar from the n'wards and an elephent's grinders of the lower jaw, represented [plate xv.]. A.B. The sea horse's head jaw, after all the flesh was taken of, measured 3 feet some odd inches, armed with many serevelas and large teeth.

The above creature when whole exceeded the largest ox in size. As for the elephent it's so well known over all Europe that it needs no discription, only there's great veriaty in the size of thier teeth, some waying 130 pounds and others 5 and 6 lbs., yet the blacks say that the smallest beast has the largest teeth.

Sunday March the 20 1758 This whole month I have had very little meterals for my Journale, otherwise then that I have indiffert. good success in the way of trade, and if it continues, I hope to be readey by the conclusian of the war to make a push for home, if all things answers acording to my expectation and no other misfortune happens to cross my purposes. However I trust in providence that I shall be able once more to reach Europe, where all my cares shall end in a happy sight of my friends and native country, which is almost the hight of my ambition. This is the 8 year since I left England or had any letters from home. As for this place I have no comfort or affection for it or its inhabatants, otherwise then it helps my fortune and puts me in a way of liveing independant at home.

Thursday March This evening I have deverted my self in so extrornery a manner that it's worthey a place in my Journale as follows. The small palm tree grows some 8 or 10 feet from the ground surounded by numerous branches from the bottom; these branches being cut away and an incision made some 3 or 4 inches in the heart of the tree, produces wine which distills from the wound for the space of 15 or 16 days and then stops—afterwards

94

the tree rots and turns to earth, which substance breeds a great quantity of worms* as thick as a man's thumb and about one inch and a qtr. long, covered over with a white skin, without hear and a large red head— these creatures are esteemed by all people here as a great danty and by some eaten raw in mouthfulls as exqusate. I have been all this evening imployed in looking for them and now have actuly the bottom of a small plate before me with some of the above wotms left after eating 5 or 6 of the largest, which I esteem before the best mutton in England. I no of nothing at home they taste so like as a broil'd rib of mutton. There's nothing is bad in them but thier shape—they have no guts, and all within is marrow produced from the old wine of the tree, which they live in untill its consum'd, then they are mittomorphid to quite another creature, by haveing wings and turns a dark colour covered over with a strong shell and looses thier fine taste.[1]

Friday March We have a set of people here that diffrt. from the Bulums in almost every circumstance of life. These are call'd Mindingo. They come from a great way inland and is a large and peoplus nation when at home. We have some of them here in the quality of magicians or southsayers, in which practicesis they shew wonders to these deluded people, by the power of evil spirits or otherwise which I don't pertend to know.

* these worms are called by the natives *bul*.

95

March the 29   I have juſt arived from the Plantains,
where I recev'd news that all the white
traders in the Sucesess has withdrawn them selves
from that river upon account of that great King or
wariour who goes by the name of* Furry Do,[1] who, as I
have said before, carrys all before him by war, invade-
ing the neibouring kingdoms and selling all he comes
at for powder and guns, which he purchaaces from the
neuterall nations.

March 30th   I have been entertain'd by an adventure
1758   that[s] worth notice as follows. Some
time ago a certain woman in labour
brought forth a sun and when her atendants brought
watter to wash the child according to cuſtum, it
cried out " Doƈter, Doƈter," which was the ocasion
of the child bearing that name. The affair was so
extrornery that I though it worthy of a place in my
Journal, tho' I thought it might be only an invention,
but upon ſtriƈt evedence I found to be trouth from
divers persons of note in the country.

Wednesday   It may perhaps be a common conjeƈture
night   of some people in the world conserning
my pressent ſtate of life as that is idle and
does no good to my fellow creatures or help the
diſtress'd, but live in indolance in a carless manner
without regard to the well fare of my county, or any
other consideration for its wellfare, which I'll endavoor

---

* Furry Do signafyes in the Mindingo language " the woman's child "
for his father is not known, a thing that verry often happens in Africa.

to clear by giveing a short discriptian of the begining
of my travils and the situation of our familey in
general. My father hinherated a good estate from my
grandfather, besides a great portsion by my mother,
but by liveing in granduour above his fortune & with
the help of a pirticular law sute, sunk him two low to
be able to provide for his children and his manner of
life lost him the affections of his frinds and relations.
In this condition we ware left to the world destatute
of any manner of relief from our old relations, who
show'd thier resentment oft, and ill will against the
children for thier parants' sake. This I found upon
my departure from Europe in the most strongest
manner imagneable, as follows. When I was revolved
to go, I paid them a visit and showed them my circumstances in the most moveing manner that I could with
modestey. They aplauded my resolution in the highest
manner and wished me a good voyage, but never once
contributed to my circumstances by a giveing hand or
shewed the least grain of pitey in my dristresses. Yet
these men lived in the hight of grandour and enjoyed
all the blessings of a plentyfull fortune even to excess.
This usage rather hightned my spirits then dejected
me, and ever since I have endavouer'd with the utmost
aplycation to live independent of these wretches, and
have found no place in all these several countrys of
England, Ireland, America, Portugall, the Caribes, the
Cape de Verd, the Azores or all the places I have been
in, I say I have found no place where I can inlarge my

97

7

fortune so soon as where I now live ; wherefore I entend to ſtay in order as before to enlarge my fortune by honeſt mains, in a country where even its beaſtly inhabatants shews me more respeﬆ then these hard-harted relations in the place of my birth. And ﬆill I can say I have never given any of them cause of offence. Here I shall do what lyes in my power to serve a countryman or any that ﬆand in need of my assiﬆance or prote﬇ion, as long as it pleases God to continue me here.

March 30
1758
Yeﬆerday my brother sail'd for the Plantains in order to sell his camwood on board of Capt. Shepherd for dry goods, who is almoﬆ readey to sail for England. Capt. Taylor is sail'd down the coaﬆ for slaves. As March is almoﬆ out our turnadoes and rains begins[1] ; therfore I entend clear away for a new plantation of muﬆurd, water melons and other things of that kind, which serves me all the rains as sallit.

April 1
1758
As I have nothing extrornery this day I have drawn the King of Sherbrow in his full majeﬆey with his gilt brass crown, siting in ﬆate over his delight, 2 pots of palm wine ; he has likewise 4 of his great lords at his feet as usial, with his trumpeter behind his chair and holding a bottle of brandy as if afreaid to set it down while he performs his office, for fear of an invession from some other quarter while he blows his blaﬆ out.

98

PLATE XVI

[face p. 98

SURRY, KING OF SHERBROW

The Island of St Anᵉ and Turtles, Plantans, Bananas and all the South Side of the river Sherbrow With Part of the Continent To the N. Ward as far as Sieralone

Saturday   I have observed that when the King is upon a visit to the Plantains, Bananas or other places, whatever town he calls at his people makes free with goats, fouls, rice, or any other necessary that they want for the bely without controwl, as a free perqusate belonging to the royal familey, which is the ocasion that the towns people hide what they can from the above imposition, as soon as the trumpit gives them notice of his arival at thier port. By what I can lern this man can't be less than 130 or 40 years of of age, his hairs is just the same as the wool of a white lamb and is depriv'd of sight; his flesh is lank and dry. These men live to a great age. You'd hardly ever find them at any other imployment then smoaking tabaco or drinking wine upon a mat under some tree half of the night and when they are extoxacated they go to sleep till morning and so on all day, while thier wives are imploy'd in in the plantation in sowing rice, miniaoca[1] and other things that the country produce. They are indeed a most thoughtless people, given to no manner of industry but just what's necessary to fill thier belys and provide a large shirt or robe to go abroad in, with a pipe as big as punch bowl and a pair of tongues about 6 inches long to lift a coal from the fire to light thier pipes, which always hangs by thier side like a dager besides thier scymiter, which I have drawn [plate xv.].

I have likewise drawn in the same page another kind of thier sword, which is commonly wore by the common sort up a good way inland, and serves to clear away bushes as well as a wapon of war.

Aprill 5th My brother's just arived from the Plantains and informs me that the Mindingo King's name is Mosolum, and that his pretence for war is because that these nations worship no god or devine being in a publick manner but live like beasts ; and in order to force them to the religion of Mahomet he has brought five thousand men well armed with bows and arows to envade thier countrys.

10th I have had a voilant favour the 5 or 6 days but it seems now to go of.

17th I am now well recovered from my favour and has this day bought a man slave, tho' I find my self at a great loss for want of a long boat to go to Sierelone in order to sell these slaves that I have now by me in the house. Now begins our trouble here on the coast, the rains is just upon us and no ships so all sell. Our hope is the castle at Bense island untill October next.

I begin to be quite tired of this country and wod run a great venture to get any way clear of it, but there are so many empedements in my way that I am afread my bones must lye here before I can find a way nome. O how I long for the produce of Europe, such as milk, sallit and a hundred other things that's good for a sick man, which I can't get here. Here I am bound up from all good conversation and even the necessarys of life. I have no satisfaction in my life and no sighns of mending it for a better now, as the war holds out on both sides. I never found myself so low in spirits since I came to Africa as this pressent time; wheather it's sickness or any distemper of body acasion'd by my late illness, I no not.

Aprill 20th We have had news here of Mr. Clow's removeall to the Turtles to live, but its not conferm'd yet.

May the 10th I have relapsd into the favour twice and is now up again. In my sickness I had the misfortune to have a prime slave run away in the middle of the day, and my man has bought a small slave that's not marchantable, so that I account my losseses in my sickness at 90 or 100 bars.

Blayney's just come from Sieralone, where the talk runs upon this great King who has almost subjued all the nations here about.

May 18 1758 This 7 or 8 days I have a dail of trouble, being just out of my sickness and visited by pilavers or black law, which was occasion'd by my gremetos, but still I am obliged to pay for it, which has reduced me very much and the loss of 2 of my people, so that I am left almost alone.

M.31 I have got 2 more men in the room of these that left me. I am in a wavouring condition as to my circumstances by the above affairs, so that I have little or nothing of any consequence to insert in my Journal, only what conserns my self as to my sickness and a longing I have to se my native

country, for I find that the expences attending a
June trader here takes away all the proffiit,
except he has a shollop, where he can
command the natives and live aboard.

There is very fue white men has the advantages we
have as to liveing, yet all is not sufficient to make any
considerable gains.

I shall fill up today with the chareƈtar of
Sunday 13*th* the mallatoes on this river. They are in a
1758
general way worse then the blacks and as
they are given to trade, which leads them into the
fashons of the English and shews them insight in the
manner we trade with the black people, our proffit is
not suffcent to satisfy them, but they make new
extortions of thier own, which renders the poor blacks
miserable a both sides. I have heard of some inƨtances
of thier cruelty, as that they have poyson'd thier own
mothers by red watter, in order to get what slaves or
affeƈts they have in thier persesion. It's easey to
consider our circumƨtances between the blacks and
melatoes and our unhappy life, which we are obliged
to lead all for the sake of riches, which at beƨt we are
not sure of in these times of wars and troubles at home
and abroad. We are afread to move one way or other
and so is miserable in both.

Wednesday These 2 or 3 days I have had several
20*th* troubles with the natives and a certain
mallato who I have mention'd in the
fore part of my Journal, who of all men bears the
worƨt of charaƈtars even with the blacks.

July 7th
1758

I have juſt arived from the Plantains with 300 and odd bars, after my loosses being the whole amount of my preſſent ſtock in dry goods.

The 10th

I am almoſt readey again for the Plantains with wood, haveing augmented my ſtock 70 bars in 3 days with the above wood.

Auguſt 23

Since the differance of the date in the margan I have been sick, so that I never had power even to walk in my house and therefore run back considerably in my ſtock, as I had no body to trade for me but the gremetoes. I have nothing else extrornery for this month, only the news that there is a Frinch schooner is taken and brought into the Plantains loaded with rum and provisions.

Auguſt 26

We have had an acount from the inland nations by a man that's truſtworthy of a terable monſter[1] kill'd by a yong man in the woods; the discriptian he gives of this creature is as follows : its body, arms and head are like a man in all things, its legs and thighs the same as an elephant and its feet like a man; it's covered over with ſtrong hair or briſtles and exceeds 2 common men in size. It's reckn'd a wonder even here where all all [*sic*] kinds of monſters are common food.

Septmr 3
1758

Ever since the above date I have been employ'd in the way of trade and yeſterday I arived from the Plantains with rum and dry goods in my long boat, where I hard the news of a small brigantine comeing up our river in order to trade for wood and slaves. She belongs to Sieralone factory and is commanded by Jubly James, who acted in the castle as second chief in former times. There is nothing more of any note since Augt. 26.

Sepmr 11
Monday The Sieralone brig is arived, to the great determent of us traders, who depends upon the good will of the natives for our trade, for the least affront now will keep them from your house, since they know there's a vessell at hand with the best of goods. I even now feel the affects of thier trade by the blacks, who if we stand hard in trade go away with the reflection that there's a vessell at hand.

Octobr I am now in a verry uncertain way; all my people has left me sick at home and 4 slaves in the house & I am not able to go anywhere to sell them. I have been in this condition ever since 20 Sepmr. and no sighns of relief, every one striveing who shall thief or steal most from me. Blayney is likewise something distress'd by the arival of a brig from Liverpool, who took two of his slaves on board in order to sell, but the sea runing too high, which made it impractable to land any thing, the capt. went down the coast and caried the 2 slaves with him, but it's to be expected he'l deliver them upon his return up again.

Octr 30*th* Capt. McCastlin of the abovemention'd brig has returnd the slaves, acording our opinion of his honestey.

104

*Novmr 2d
1758*
Yesterday arived from Liverpool the Bee Sno, Capt. Potter, where I have sould 3 slaves, but has not receved all my goods yet upon account of the bad surf and bar. I expect to come by some losses as to weting my goods before they are all landed safe. I have hired some more gremetoes and find myself groeing better every day as to my health. I am likewise prapareing for action again and exercise.

In this manner we spend the prime of youth among negroes, scrapeing the world for money, the uneversal god of man kind, untill death overtakes us.

Novmr 10
Capt. Potter's boat has been here and I have sould the mate, Mr. Eaton, one prime man slave—in all to Capt. Potter 4 slaves, for which I receved 260 ship's bars, one of them not being prime. I have now in the house between 3 and 400 ships bars, but not very well assorted as to lead and iron, and some other things of less note.

25th
Capt. Potter's mate has been here and bought one slave from Mr. Tucker. Nothing else extrornery at present. He is gone again down to Mana for trade. As usial this month there is no trade stiring.

January 4
The last month has passed over without any busness as to trade. I am still in a lingering way of sickness and can't recover my former strength. I have likewise some troubles as to my

people, who has left me, all but 2 boys, the same time I am building a new house.

We have the secret news that the old King of Sherbrow's dead but is not yet spred abroad, according to thier usual custum of keeping thier disseased kings a good while hid, in order to make a new one before any troubles ensues.

I have never seen such a scarse time of trade on the coast since I have known it as this pressent time—I have not bought any trade this 2 months, not so much as a serevela. I still long more and more for a return to my native country.

Janr 27 My house is not finished yet so that I am in great distress ; as I am not able to look for trade my self and has no body to send makes my case the more miserable. I find my stock lessen'd about 100 bars since 3 months' time. There is a vessell from New England arived at Sieralone.

Febery 3 1758 Lately we have the malloncoly news of Capt. Potter's being cut of by the slaves at Mano and the ship drove ashoar ; the captain, second mate & docter are all killed in a barbarous manner by the slaves. The slaves are all taken by the natives again and sould to other vessells, so that they have nothing mended thier condition by thier enterprize.

Feb 12 Mr. Tucker's sons has arived from Cape Mount, with several articles belonging to Capt. Potter's vessell that hove on shoar.

finish'd.

106

[*From this point the Diary is continued by Blayney Owen*].

March This fatal month makes the final period of the author's life, who died the 26 of this month, who left me to struggle with the world a little longer, disconsolate & alone amidst negroes. No man can be ignorant of my affliction in the said circumstances, tho' in want of nothing, I mean the necessarys of life. My chief trust is in the Almighty, Who of His great mercy has given me a tranquillity of mind which is above what this world can give, & which alone sustains me amid the tempestuous waves of my severe affliction. He teaches me to look att every Christian as my brother and supply the place of the deceas'd which is some comfort to me, altho' it is but an imperfect imitation of his fraternall affection.

Am very disconsolate, which is heighten'd by my solitude, which makes me resolve to go to the Plantans & see Mr. Clow.

This month trade is plenty; I have given Capt. Brookbank about 5½ tons camwood & Mr. Clow 2½ this 2 mths.

April 25 I'm taken verry ill of a severe fever this 2 or three days, which I'm afraid will last long, as I'm almost sure of haveing a fitt of sickness every tornado times, as they are coming on verry fast.

May This 5 days last past am verry ill of the fever, having lost all appetite, which with my late misfortunes, has brought me verry low, my

107

only refuge left is God, Who alone is able to support me under afflictions.

I have got the better of my late illness & am beginning to stir about buisness.

June   Nothing remarkable, but Capt. Howel's arrivall at the Plaintans with a verry bad assortment.

Trade is pretty brisk; I have gone two or three times to Plaintans with Camwood; there is also a vessell from the factory arrivd att Yorkisland for wood & slaves, commanded by Alexdr. Taylor. The 29th of this month there happen'd the greatest storm of thunder & lightning I have seen since I've been in Africa; for the space of 3 hours it lighten'd prodigiously, being in fear of our houses blown up every minute on acct. of the powder in them.

NOTES TO THE TEXT.

[1] *Page 21.* This date was evidently first written as 1756, and then " 8 " has been superimposed.

[2] *Page 21.* For an account of Owen's Irish connections see p. 96.

[1] *Page 22.* The group of the West Indies from Porto Rico to Trinidad.

[2] *Page 22.* Bryan Edwards in his *History, Civil and Commercial, of the British Colonies and the West Indies,* published in 1793-4, also writes of this Irish population in Montserrat, which he says had come in in the seventeenth century, and consisted partly of adventurers from St. Kitts, and partly of other Irish Roman Catholics who had joined their co-religionists there.

[3] *Page 22.* Peter Kalm in *Travels into North America* describes a voyage from Gravesend to Philadelphia in 1748 which lasted " not quite 41 days " as " reckoned one of the shortest, for it is common in winter-time to be 14 or more weeks in coming from Gravesend to Philadelphia." See Pinkerton, *General Collection of Voyages*, XIII, 386.

[1] *Page 23.* Owen's notes of latitude and longitude are not to be relied on for accuracy. They are approximate only.

[1] *Page 24.* " Elephants' teeth " was the name generally used for tusks in the ivory trade.

[2] *Page 24.* See note 2, p. 36.

[1] *Page 27.* Another form of the word is *cassava*. It is a tuberous root very much used for food by the natives. On the varieties of cassava near this region, see J. D. Hooker, *Flora Nigritiana* (1849), 509.

[2] *Page 27.* As there are no tigers in this region the tracks which frightened Owen were possibly those of a leopard.

[1] *Page 28.* The " Oister Isle " here is apparently a synonym for one of the Turtle Islands. There is no sign of an island marked " Oyster Isle " nearer than the Camaranca River, which is too far away to be the island referred to here.

[2] *Page 28.* The English factory at Sierra Leone, which was situated on Bence Island, had belonged to the Royal African Company, but having been abandoned by the Company in 1728 a group of private traders had taken possession of it and an Act of Parliament in 1752 confirmed their claims. See 25 Geo. II, C. 40, Clause III.

¹ *Page 29.* Another traveller to this region, one William Smith, who published *A New Voyage to Guinea in* 1744, stated that these plantains were called " *Indian figs* " and believed to be the figs of Scripture because "the leaves are prodigious, large and broad, consequently much fitter to make aprons of than are fig leaves."

² *Page 29.* Papas or popow : the fruit of the *carica papaya*. Sir Harry Johnston describes the fruit as " a very good imitation of a hothouse melon." *Liberia*, p. 536.

³ *Page 29.* The description which Owen gives of the Bulloms and their customs is borne out by other writers on the tribe. See T. Winterbottom, *An Account of the Native Africans in the neighbourhood of Sierra Leone*, 1803.

⁴ *Page 29.* These mulattos, a half-caste race part European, part negro, took an important share in the trade of the coast. Owen gives an unfavourable description of their character on p. 102, an account which pales before that given by William Smith whose mildest expression about them was " a parcel of the most profligate villans neither true to the negroes nor to one another." *op. cit*, p. 218.

¹ *Page 30.* This figure 3 does not appear anywhere in the Journal. Reason for missing illustrations is given on page 91.

² *Page 30.* Winterbottom, *op. cit.*, pp. 129-133, gives a detailed account of the red-water trial which he considers a variety of trial by ordeal. Owen gives further details on p. 54.

³ *Page 30.* This Bullom secret society is described by Mr. Northcote Thomas in his *Anthropological Report on Sierra Leone* (1916), Part I, 143 *seq.* His account does not vary in any essential detail from Owen's. The attempt to reproduce the cry made by the Poramen which Owen gives as " wo pon," is made by Mr. Northcote Thomas as " O pon."

¹ *Page 32.* An edible lizard. Winterbottom classifies it as *lacerta iguana* (*op. cit.*, p. 69).

² *Page 32.* There is no sign of a long worm in any illustration.

¹ *Page 33.* A pilot was needed as there was a dangerous bar at the mouth of the River Gambia.

² *Page 33.* Gourds used as vessels for holding liquids.

³ *Page 33.* Hides were a considerable article for export from West Africa. The English exported them from their Gambia factories.

⁴ *Page 33.* Moydore or moidore was a Portuguese gold coin, which according to Wyndham Beawes was worth £1 7s. in 1761. See his *Lex Mercatoria*, 886.

[1] *Page* 34. Beeswax was another article of the English export trade from the Gambia.

[2] *Page* 34. The Western Isles was a name for the Azores.

[1] *Plate* vi. The Portuguese in the sixteenth and seventeenth centuries had attempted conversion of the natives through the work of the Order of Christ and of Franciscans, Austins and Dominicans. Native converts were encouraged to live apart from the other inhabitants, and the nunnery here referred to, which had evidently passed into secular hands, had probably been a missionary centre. See Lannoy and Vander Linden : *Histoire de l'expansion des peuples européennes.* It is not clear whether the " black " refers to the order of nuns or to their colour.

[1] *Page* 36. The crown here is a Portuguese silver coin worth 2s. 8d. in 1761. See Wyndham Beawes, *op. cit.* 881.

[2] *Page* 36. The use of the " bar " as a recognised medium of exchange occurs frequently in the accounts of those who traded in Guinea in the eighteenth century. Dr. Winterbottom made calculations as to the value of the bar. "From Senegal to Cape Mesurado on the Windward Coast as it is called, the medium of computation is termed a bar, hence the trade is named the *bar trade.* . . . The bar, which is the current medium round Sierre Leone, is like one pound sterling, merely nominal, but even less precise in its value, and subject to great irregularities. Moreover the quantity of an article contained in a bar differs, not only on various parts of the coast, but often in neighbouring rivers. A gun valued at twenty shillings is sold for six bars ; but the same number of bars of tobacco will only be equal in value to four or five shillings. Twenty leaves of tobacco are a bar ; and a gallon of rum or a fathom of chintz pass for no more. A piece of cloth which in one place passes for six bars, passes in others for eight, and in others for ten. Hence the trader, in disposing of his goods, forms to himself a standard to which upon the average he reduces all his bars, the number of cheap bars which he sells serving to diminish the value of the dearer kind " (*op. cit.*, 172-3).

[3] *Page* 36. Other forms of the word are archil or orchil : a lichen used to make a violet dye. There was keen rivalry among European countries in attempts to secure dye stuffs in the seventeenth and eighteenth centuries. This Portuguese attempt to prevent English traders from securing archil is paralleled by the English restriction on the export of indigo and camwood.

⁴ *Page* 36. The Danish trade with China developed when their East India Company received a new Charter in 1728. Macpherson states that in 1747 of twenty European ships trading in China two were Danish. *Annals of Commerce* III, 259. Lannoy and Van der Linden consider that this pursuit of the Chinese trade was carried on at the expense of the Danish India trade. *Histoire de l'expansion des peuples européens.*

¹ *Page* 37. This was a very common native practice on the Guinea Coast. A native who considered himself injured by a European of any nation took his revenge on the next European who appeared a suitable victim, although he might be quite unconnected with the crime.

¹ *Page* 38. The dollar here is the Spanish piece of 8 *reals* which was commonly used in the American colonies before their separation from England and called a dollar. Beawes, *op. cit.*, reports the Spanish dollar in 1761 worth " an uncertain number of pence."

¹ *Page* 39. The gromettos were a most important group of free blacks, who did service on the vessels trading along the coast.

² *Page* 39. The island of Goree was an important trading centre and was fought for at different times by Portuguese, Dutch, French and English. It had passed to France by the treaty of Nymwegen, and at the time of this entry it was their chief trading base, on the African coast, protected by a fort. It was captured by an English naval and military force in 1758, but the news of its fall does not appear to have reached Owen.

³ *Page* 39. Isle of May : the island of Maio, in the Cape Verde Islands.

⁴ *Page* 39. The only illustration of Fogo is a plate *vii.*

¹ *Page* 41. Silesias : a fine linen material manufactured in Silesia.

¹ *Page* 43. The English castle was the fort on James Island in the Gambia under the management of either the Royal African Company, or the Company of Merchants trading to Africa, depending upon what the missing year of the adventure was.

² *Page* 43. Anglicé sheds.

¹ *Page* 44. *Natives* as catchword at foot of page.

¹ *Page* 45. River of Renonas : the Rio Nunez.

² *Page* 45. For an explanation of this sum, see note 2, p. 36. Though according to Owen's calculation here four guns equal 20 country bars or 16 ship's bars, and therefore one ship's bar would appear to equal $1\frac{1}{4}$ country bars, one silk handkerchief

is worth one country bar *or* one ship's bar. And while the cost of a head of beads would make the value of a country bar appear to be 3s. 4d., when reckoned in terms of a dozen knives it is 4s. 6d. The exhausted mathematician may well echo Dr. Winterbottom : " It would tend greatly to facilitate commercial intercourse . . . were this fluctuating medium of bars abolished."

[1] *Page* 46. Coarse cotton material brought from the East Indies to England and re-exported to Guinea.

[2] *Page* 46. The figures here have been altered : the brass pans cost either 1 bar 2s. 8d., or 1 bar 1s. 6d.

[3] *Page* 46. Quentall : the measure of a hundredweight, 112 lbs.

[1] *Page* 47. I have not been able to trace the island of St. Ann. It is not marked on the Admiralty Charts of the region, or on the contemporary maps that I have been able to consult. Possibly it is one of the Turtle Islands off Cape St. Anne.

[1] *Page* 49. Palaver, from the Portuguese *palavra*, was the common name for a meeting for argument or conference which followed disputes on the coast. Those concerned in the quarrel with their supporters met to discuss terms of agreement. There are instances of Englishmen being invited to preside over these meetings on the Gold Coast, where the English authority was stronger, but even there the judgment was according to native custom.

[1] *Page* 50. Other forms of the word are gree-gree and gri-gri, a European name for the amulets worn by the natives of this region. Lieut. John Matthews, in his *Voyage to the River Sierra Leone*, 1788, gives a fuller description of them. " These are made of goatskin, either with the hair on, or dresst like Morocco leather, into various shapes and sizes, from the bigness of a shilling to the size and form of a sheep's heart, and stuffed with some kind of powder, and bits of paper on which are written in Arabic sentences from the Alcoran ; these they wear tied round their necks, waist, legs and arms, and in such numbers that where a man is properly equipped for the field, the very weight of them with his gun is an exceeding heavy burden."

[1] *Page* 51. The virtues of this nut, *kola acuminata*, are given at length in a report on the Botany and Geology of Sierra Leone drawn up by G. F. Scott-Elliott and Miss C. A. Raisin in 1893. " The following are some of its properties. A nut or even half a nut will enable one to go without food and support great fatigue for twenty-four hours or more. It is an excellent nerve

tonic. . . . A property not understood is that of rapidly clearing foul water and improving beer. It is said to remove immediately and thoroughly the unsteadiness and stupidity due to drunkenness."

² *Page* 51. See below, note 1, p. 95.

¹ *Page* 52. Winterbottom writes of a musical instrument which may perhaps be the one referred to here. He calls it the *banja* and quoting Bryan-Edwards says that it is like an imperfect kind of violincello.

¹ *Page* 53. The name of this tribe is variously reproduced in English. R. H. Cust, *A Sketch of the Modern Languages of Africa* (1883) gives it as Temne or Timmani, and Dr. Northcote Thomas, *op. cit.*, as Timne. Owen speaks of the Timne as being a distant tribe lying far inland, but Mr. Winterbottom wrote in 1803 they had reached the sea-coast on the south side of the river Sierra Leone, having extended their boundaries at the expense of the Bulloms. They are a pagan and warlike race.

² *Page* 53. As there is no exhaustive and definite history of the tribes of this region, and as there has been considerable tribal migration since the eighteenth century, it is not possible to trace these three "nations" with certainty. The Ordnance Survey Map of Sierra Leone, published in 1921, shows *Banta* as a tribal region near the upper reaches of the Jong and Bagru rivers. *Kono* is mentioned by R. N. Cust, *op. cit*, p. 185, as the language of a small tribe adjacent to the Temne near Sierra Leone, and *Tene* as a "small language" spoken on the Rio Nunez, *op. cit.*, 181.

¹ *Page* 54. I have found no other authority for the existence of these Amazons.

² *Page* 54. Camwood, a hard red wood, *baphia nitida*, was used in the production of a dye as well as for furniture making, and hence very much valued.

³ *Page* 54. See note 2, page 30.

¹ *Page* 55. See infra note 1, page 57.

¹ *Page* 57. The Mandingos were a conquering race from the region of the Upper Niger. They adopted the Mohammedan religion, but spread their conquest over races some of which, like the Bulloms, remained pagan. The Mandingo powers of divination seem to have disturbed Owen's mind, but his conclusion that the diviners were in league with devils restored his balance "since we have examples in all ages of the power of witchcraft" (see p. 90).

² *Page* 57.   The Koran.

¹ *Page* 58.   There is no sign of a sketch of York Island.

² *Page* 58.   This river appears as the *Deong* in a contemporary map in a collection called the *Africa Pilot*, 1799, but nineteenth century maps give it as *Jong*.   See map at end of volume.

¹ and ² *Page* 59.   I have not been able to trace either Berebosa's town or the province of Oddfa.

¹ *Page* 60.   Shalop is a variant of sloop.

² *Page* 60.   Slabar sauce is a sauce of palm-oil mixed with pepper and various other ingredients.

¹ *Page* 61.   Laffers are so called from the Arabic word, *laffa*, a cover.

¹ *Page* 64.   The date 1756 is probably a slip.   See page 69, where the marginal date is March 1756.

¹ *Page* 68.   The " New Lights " and " Old Lights " here referred to were two parties in the Presbyterian Church in Philadelphia who had divided in 1739 on the subject of the education of candidates for the ministry.   An account of their discussions is given by C. A. Briggs in *American Presbyterianism* (1885).

¹ *Page* 69.   The engagement here mentioned at Crown Point on Lake Champlain is the victory of colonial forces under Sir William Johnson over the French under Diesku in July, 1755.

² *Page* 69.   The Dembia River ; its mouth is just North of the Isles de Los.

³ *Page* 69.   The Susses, or Susus, were like the Mandingoes, (see note 1, page 57 above), a warring and successful tribe who had extended their boundaries at the expense of their neighbours. Their territory lay between the Rio Nunez and the river Scarcies.

⁴ *Page* 69.   The more usual form of the word on contemporary maps is Bisseo or Bissao.   It was the site of a Portuguese fort at the mouth of the river Geba.

⁵ *Page* 69.   This earthquake took place on 1st November, 1755.   The Portuguese Royal Family were at Balam when the disaster occurred.

¹ *Page* 72.   The occasional attempt of a captain in haste to leave the coast to secure his cargo by kidnapping free negroes always roused protest among the regular traders, who were then liable to suffer for this sin, as Owen himself had done. See above, p. 37.

² *Page* 72.   14th March, 1757.

[1] *Page* 73. Screvelos or Scrivelloes was the name used in trade for tusks below a certain weight. See A. Maskell, *Ivory in Commerce and in the Arts, Cantor Lectures*, 1906, who gives " below about 7 lbs." as the mark of scrivelloes.

[2] *Page* 73. Pompion is a pumpkin—*cucurbita pepo*, see Elliott and Raisin, *op. cit.*, p. 43.

[3] *Page* 73. Possibly the pigeon pea : *cajanus indicus*.

[1] *Page* 79. The chameleon seems to have aroused the interest of most travellers to Guinea. Accounts of it are given by Bosman, Snelgrove, Winterbottom, William Smith and many others.

[1] *Page* 80. Date repeated.

[2] *Page* 80. A similar complaint was made by the officers of the Company of Merchants trading to Africa, who were faced with what they considered impossible odds in being left to maintain the English forts without naval help at a time when lack of trading vessels was ruining their position in the eyes of the natives.

[3] *Page* 80. These ships were sent out in accordance with the provisions of the Act of 1752 which provided for the maintenance of the English forts by the new Company subject to the inspection of men of war to be sent out by the Admiralty.

[1] *Page* 81. There is a missing leaf here, so that the nature of the creature who so badly frightened Owen remains a matter of conjecture.

[1] *Page* 82. These men-of-war had arrived on the coast in August in response to the appeals for protection for the trading interest.

It is strange that while Owen comments on the arrival of this small force, he fails to make any mention of the great land and sea attack on the French trading forts at Senegal, which took place in the spring of 1758 and resulted in the capture of Fort Louis and Goree.

[2] *Page* 82. The news is no doubt that of the disasters of the summer campaign of 1757—the defeat of Frederick at Kolin in June and of the Duke of Cumberland at Hastenbeck in July.

[1] *Page* 83. *Vide supra*, p. 69.

[1] *Page* 84. The manatee is common in the rivers and estuaries of West Africa. Sir Harry Johnston points out that there has been confusion between manatee and hippo, but Owen is clear that the beast he means is the manatee proper, as he mentions its want of feet.

² *Page* 84. Winterbottom denied the existence of cannibalism in this part of Africa, *op. cit.*, 166-167. "That this horrid practice does not exist in the neighbourhood of Sierra Leone, nor for many hundred leagues along the coast to the Northward and Southward of that place, may be asserted with the utmost confidence, nor is there any tradition among the natives which can prove it ever was the custom ; on the contrary they appear struck with horror when they are questioned individually on the subject though at the same time they make no scruple of accusing other natives at a distance and whom they barely know by name of cannibalism."

¹ *Page* 87. I have not been able to trace any allusion to this affair in the Parliamentary records. The taking up of the case of an aggrieved trading captain by the Commons is not incredible, but it appears unlikely at this time.

¹ *Page* 89. I have not succeeded in tracing this interesting creature. Owen's indiscriminate use of the word "worm" for all kinds of creeping things makes some of his observations hard to follow.

¹ *Page* 93. There is no account of Mandigo kings, except Stokvis's list in his *Manuel d'histoire, de généalogie et de chronologie* (1888-93), p. 472, which ends in 1390, so that this king "Furry Do" or King "Musolum" as he is called on page 100 cannot be traced.

² *Page* 93. This repulsive spider is described by other travellers. William Smith, *op. cit.* 157, gives a similar account of it. Sir Harry Johnston points out that it serves a useful purpose in destroying insects.

¹ *Page* 95. It seems evident that these "worms" are the larvæ of a beetle which eats into the palm trees. Sir Harry Johnston (*op. cit.*, p. 851) writes that the grubs of the destructive *passalidæ* family of beetles are a favourite article of diet with the natives of Liberia.

¹ *Page* 96. See p. 93.

¹ *Page* 98. Tornado seasons in Sierra Leone were from April to June, and October and November, according to Dr. Winterbottom.

¹ *Page* 99. Miniaoca or manioc is another name for cassava. See note 1, p. 27, above.

¹ *Page* 103. Probably a chimpanzee, of which there are several varieties in this part of Africa.

INDEX TO THE JOURNAL